Photogravure Goupil & Cie

Yours very Truly
Alfred Hutton

ALFRED HUTTON

COLD STEEL

The Art of Fencing with the Sabre

Introduction by
RAMON MARTINEZ

DOVER PUBLICATIONS, INC., MINEOLA, NEW YORK

Bibliographical Note

This Dover edition, first published in 2006, is an unabridged republication of *Cold Steel: A Practical Treatise on the Sabre*, published by William Clowes and Sons, Limited, London, 1889. A new introduction has been specially prepared for this edition. In addition, most of the plates have been backed up, but maintain the same general position they had in the original text.

Library of Congress Cataloging-in-Publication Data

Hutton, Alfred.
Cold steel : the art of fencing with the sabre / Alfred Hutton ; introduction by Ramon Martinez.
p. cm.
Reprint. Originally published: London : William Clowes and Sons, 1889.
ISBN-13: 978-0-486-44931-9 (pbk.)
ISBN-10: 0-486-44931-9 (pbk.)
1. Sabers. 2. Fencing. I. Title.

U860.H875 2006
796.86—dc22

2006040016

Manufactured in the United States by LSC Communications
44931910 2020
www.doverpublications.com

TO

My Friend

EGERTON CASTLE, F.S.A.

CONTENTS.

THE SABRE.

THE SABRE—*continued.*

LIST OF PLATES.

INTRODUCTION TO THE DOVER EDITION

Over a century ago in Victorian England, Captain Alfred Hutton, career military officer, teacher of swordsmanship, historian, and antiquarian, observed the state of fencing in England (particularly sabre fencing) and concluded that it was in a sad state—or, to use his own words, the direction it was taking was "distinctly retrograde."

Captain Hutton's book *Cold Steel*, published in 1889, sought to offer a solution to this perceived decay in the art of fencing. Part of his solution involved the development of his own unique system of sabre fencing, employing a weapon made to his own specifications. This lightweight weapon was similar to those used in European fencing academies of his time, especially in Italy. In Hutton's opinion, this type of sabre offered more variety and finesse of technique than the clumsy, heavier weapon still being used in the English schools.

In the book, Hutton states that the system he created and advocates is based on "Old English backsword play of the eighteenth century combined with the 'modern Italian school.'" However, there is much more to his method, as his system also contains elements and techniques of Italian rapier fencing, French foil, and smallsword. Hutton makes this eclectic approach evident throughout his treatise by incorporating techniques of the old masters and making many references to their treatises to support the use of such historical methods in his system. These methods and techniques include using the pommel of the sabre to strike the adversary in the face and "commanding"—that is, seizing the person and/or weapon of the adversary with the unarmed hand. All of these were commonly subjects of instruction in the days when men carried swords at their hips and knowing how to use one's sidearm could be a matter of life or death.

In essence, Alfred Hutton based his methods of swordsmanship on the fundamentals of the French school of fencing, in which he received his early instruction at the famous school of Angelo. This institution of London society had been founded in the eighteenth century, and operated continuously through the nineteenth century until it finally closed in 1897. Hutton observed from his own experience and historical sources, the advantages of beginning with the foil and then proceeding to learn the use of the sabre. He admits and includes the use of all of the foil parries in his system of sabre fencing and commences his instruction upon the premise that the pupil is already well versed in the use of the foil.

Hutton's system has often been thought to be a relatively simple system of "military" sabre fencing. However, a meticulous reading of *Cold Steel* shows that nothing could be further from the truth. Hutton's unique system of sabre fencing is neither civilian nor military, and cannot be relegated solely to the floor of the *salle d'armes*, or thought of as a weapon to be used only in time of war. His system of sabre fencing could have been used on the dueling field, the battlefield, or as a method of self-defense.

As a professional military man, teacher of fencing, accomplished swordsman, and fencer since his youth, Hutton realized the value and importance of training in fencing for military personnel; however, he was also cognizant that the methods and training learned in schools of fencing could not be directly applied on the battlefield exactly as they were taught and practiced in the schools. Nevertheless, Hutton felt that they served as a strong foundation upon which combative methods and techniques could be developed for fighting in earnest where the purpose was to stop the enemy by hurting, maiming or killing. For Hutton, fencing was the queen of all athletic endeavor. Besides being one of the best methods of exercise for physical conditioning and maintenance of a sound physique and health, this type of training, more importantly, provided practice in instant decision-making, strategic thinking, and tactical considerations. Furthermore, the practice of fencing against a wide variety of training partners provided opportunities to cultivate an acute comprehension of hand-to-hand combat—the very essence of being a soldier and warrior. In Hutton's unmechanized age, even an officer might have to engage physically with the enemy. The attributes honed on the floors of the fencing schools thus provided tools that no career military officer could afford to be without.

Hutton's sound thinking on this point is shown in the sections in *Cold Steel* devoted to the use of the sabre when facing a soldier armed with a bayonet. He even goes so far as to include a section on the use of the sabre when facing a man armed with the French sword. Although Hutton realized that this sort of practice was obsolete, since thrusting swords of this type were no longer carried in his time, it nevertheless provided a method for both swordsmen to test themselves and their skills of judgment, strategy, and tactical application. Hutton also delves into the use of other weapons whose methods of use he also incorporated in the training and practice of fencing, including the French dueling sword, the great stick, the constable's truncheon, and the short sword-bayonet or dagger. In discussing all of the weapons covered in his book, the author adheres to the theory and practice of fencing, which he viewed in all his writings as the basis for obtaining a complete comprehension of armed combat.

Alfred Hutton devoted much of his life to the revitalization of fencing in Britain, and the comprehensive treatment given to the sabre and other weapons in *Cold Steel* was intended to bring the art and science of these weapons up to date with his times. This republication will, I hope, show Hutton's system to be equally relevant to our own age. It is therefore with great satisfaction and enthusiasm that I present again one of the most well-known and well-received texts on the skillful management of the sabre. I hope that all contemporary aficionados of the sabre delight in this book as much as I have.

Maestro Ramon Martinez
President, Association for Historical Fencing
Founding Member, International Masters at Arms Federation
Director, Martinez Academy of Arms

COLD STEEL.

THE SABRE.

INTRODUCTION.

THE art of the Broadsword or Sabre has developed and improved rapidly in foreign schools during the present century, whereas in England progress has been but slight, even if we can be said to have progressed at all, as any one must allow who has perused the works of such masters of the eighteenth century, as Hope, M'Bane, James Miller, Lonnergan, and Roworth, the latter of whom, together with Mr. Angelo, seems to owe his knowledge of this weapon to John Taylor, a well-known broadsword master, who taught the Light Horse Volunteers of London and Westminster in 1798.

Quite lately, indeed, our movement has been distinctly retrograde, the efforts of our military swordsmen being so entirely confined to the simplification of their method of instruction as to preclude the introduction of anything in the shape of variety of play; and it is in the hope of arresting this retrogression that I venture to offer the following pages to the fencing public.

I base my system partly on the instruction I received in early life in the school of Messrs. Angelo, and partly on certain very lucid Italian works of the present day, combined with matter extracted from the writings of the English masters of the last century—a period in which the "backsword" was held in much esteem as a typical English weapon, its art was highly cultivated, and it was moreover largely employed in the stage prize-fights.

The arm I recommend for school-practice is a *light sabre* similar to those used on the Continent, which, from its slight weight, is capable of more varied treatment than the cumbersome weapons in vogue in our English schools.

As regards the *helmet*, the wirework of the face should be close, like that of a fencing mask, and at the same time very strong, in order to prevent any accidental penetration by the narrow sword-blade.

The Parts of the Sabre.

The sabre consists of two principal parts—the blade and the hilt.

The blade is divided into three parts:—the *tang*, the narrow piece of soft metal which fits into the hilt; the *forte*, the half of the blade nearest to the hilt, with which all cuts and points are parried; and the *foible*, the half nearest the point, with which all attacks are made.

We must further observe the edge, the back, and the "false" edge—that sharp part of the back which extends from the point to the place where the grooving usually begins, a distance of about eight inches—the use of which nowadays is so little understood in England even by the masters themselves, but which the Italian fencers understand so well and use so deftly.

At the period of the Renaissance, when fencing in European countries may be said to have taken its rise, the entire back of the rapier, the weapon then in vogue, was termed "falso," and was used for both parrying and cutting equally with the true edge.

The *hilt* consists of the *shell*, which protects the hand; the *grip*, which the hand grasps; and the *pummel*, the lump of steel at the extreme end, which is of sufficient size and weight to balance the sword.

How to Hold the Sabre.

The fingers must be lightly but firmly closed round the grip, with the thumb extended along the back of it, the centre knuckles being in the same line as the edge; the thumb may, however, sometimes be shifted in order to relieve the hand, and placed round the grip, similarly to the fingers.

GUARD.

The *guard* is that position of body and sword which is the most safe for defence, and the most ready for attack; and care must be taken not to confuse the term, as has often been done, with that of the "parade" or "parry," which is a distinctly defensive movement for the purpose of stopping a cut or thrust.

Fencing masters, I think, all agree that it is highly advantageous to the beginner to study the use of the foil, before proceeding to cultivate that of the sabre, and such has most certainly been my own personal experience.

Lonnergan, one of the most reliable and complete writers of the "backsword" period, remarks in his work of 1771, 'The Fencer's Guide,' "The man well instructed first in the small sword will be so habituated to a nicety of disengaging, that he must conserve it in some measure for ever after; and thus, by this first impression, will be yet more nice in catching at the many openings proceeding from the wide disengagements of the backsword play than even his master, if ignorant of the small. If the back is first learned, the wrist will be in danger of being incapable of due command in the exercise of the small sword for ever after." I shall therefore infer that the pupil is so far proficient in the lessons of the foil, as to understand the correct

PLATE I.

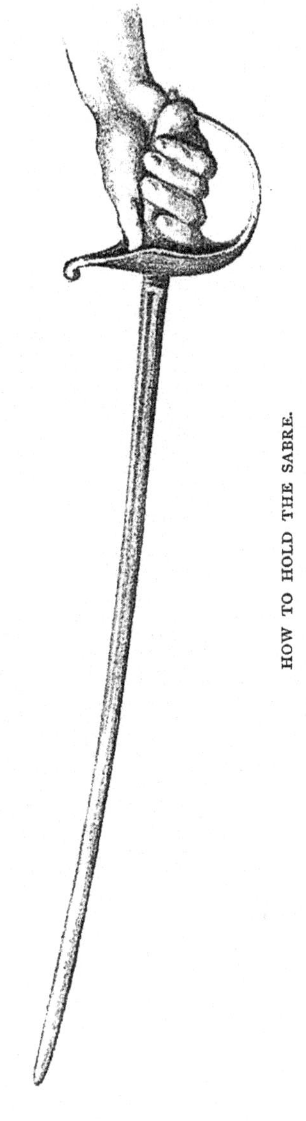

HOW TO HOLD THE SABRE.

PLATE II.

FIRST POSITION.

positions of the guard and the lunge, as also the parries used in foil fencing, all of which I use more or less in my present system. These parries it may be as well to recapitulate; they are: quarte, tierce, septime, seconde, prime, sixte, and octave; the two latter parries enter but little into sabre practice.

1st Position—i. e. before coming on Guard.

The sabre is to be gripped as before directed. The body and legs to be as in the similar position in foil practice.

The left hand to be closed, and to rest on the left hip; the sword arm lowered, edge to the right, the point to the front and directed diagonally towards the ground, and the nails down, that is, in the position called "pronation."

The Guards.

The old masters taught four engaging guards as a general rule, though one or two others are also mentioned in their works, viz. Inside, Outside, Medium, and the Hanging Guard. The feet, when on guard, must be in a similar position to that of "guard" in Foil fencing.

The *Inside Guard* is in the form of Quarte.

The *Outside Guard* is in the form of Tierce.

The *Medium* is neither Quarte nor Tierce, but, as its name suggests, is immediately between the two, the edge being inclined downwards, and the point opposite to the opponent's face.

The *Hanging Guard* is to a certain extent a "Prime." It is formed by dropping the point to a level with the opponent's right hip, raising the hand as high as the head, the edge to be uppermost—and looking at the opponent under the shell of the sword. This guard is useful mainly as a shelter to retreat under in recovering after having made an attack; and it should be always so used, whether the attack has been successful or not; as there are some swordsmen who, either from nervousness or from evil disposition, invariably strike again instead of acknowledging after they have received a palpable and fair hit.

Of these the Tierce, and *especially the Medium*, which is nothing more than the "Guardia Mista" of Alfieri (1640), are the best for the combined purposes of defence and attack, because in these positions the arm is least likely to become fatigued, and it is on this Medium Guard that I shall, following the advice of practical old Alfieri, base all my ensuing lessons.

The *High Seconde*, or, as some call it, the "low hanging guard," is very much in vogue at present, especially in the military gymnasia. It is not a recent invention, as I find it in the 'Fechtkunst' of Johann

PLATE III.

MEDIUM GUARD.

PLATE IV.

THE INSIDE GUARD—AFTER JAMES MILLER, 1737.

Andrea Schmidt (1713), also in Girard's work (1736), and Angelo (1763). These authors show the small sword working successfully against it, and as the works of these writers were dedicated to that weapon principally, they naturally showed the unfortunate "espadonneur" in the worst position they could place him in; it was evidently not used by the backswordmen. It has the same disadvantage as the "Hanging Guard" in causing unnecessary fatigue to the arm, which is raised about as high as the shoulder, thereby keeping the deltoid muscle, which is by no means a strong one, in a state of constant tension.

There is yet another Guard, in the form of *Sixte*. The point being carried a little above the horizontal line, and sometimes a little depressed below it, the sword is carried well to the right, so as to cover the outside; and from it cuts outside the leg, at the right side or right cheek, may be parried with the back of the sword in *Sixte* or *Octave*. I find this guard very useful against the High Seconde, as it is a position to which the high seconde player is quite unused. It is recommended by Lonnergan, and also by Captain Godfrey in his interesting work, which appeared in 1747, in which he describes it as having been much used by a celebrated old "gladiator" of the early part of that century, named Perkins, who, as he states, although an old man, and stiff from age, was wont to puzzle with it even so great a man as Figg, "the Atlas of the sword," himself.

The Resting Medium.

Lower the sword hand until the pummel rests on the thigh about six or eight inches above the knee.

This position is useful during a long encounter, when the opponent is out of reach—the arm being in repose will be the more ready for vigorous action when required.

PLATE V.

THE OUTSIDE GUARD—AFTER JAMES MILLER, 1737.

PLATE VI.

THE HANGING GUARD—AFTER JAMES MILLER, 1737.

PLATE VII

THE ST. GEORGE'S GUARD—AFTER JAMES MILLER, 1737.

THE ATTACK.

THE "MOULINET."

A VERY old exercise is this, for the purpose of gaining strength and flexibility in the wrist, the point whence all the cuts should in the main proceed; it has been recommended, in forms more or less complete, by most good masters, from the days of Giacomo di Grassi, A.D. 1570.

It consists of six cuts, the first, a diagonal cut downward from right to left; the second, diagonal downward from left to right; the third, diagonal upward from right to left; the fourth, diagonal upward from left to right; the fifth, horizontal from right to left; and the sixth, horizontal from left to right.

To assist the beginner, a target, either oval or circular, and about 14 inches in diameter, should be fixed on the wall, about as high as a man's shoulder, having drawn on it two diagonal lines, and one horizontal line passing through its centre; these lines indicate the course which the six cuts are to take. The pattern which I think the most preferable is that given by Roworth.

The swordsman should stand on guard (medium) a few feet from the target.

Moulinet 1.

Motion 1.—Extend the sword arm completely, the hand to be in quarte, and the point a little raised, the hilt of the sword being about the height of the chin, and the edge directed obliquely downwards to the left.

Motion 2.—Drop the point diagonally downwards from right to left, taking care that the edge leads during the passage of the blade along the line on the target; then allow the wrist to revolve so as to bring the thumb downwards, and the back of the hand and the flat of the blade opposite your left side, and cause the sword to describe a complete circle, thereby bringing it again to the position described in the first motion.

This moulinet, as likewise all the others, must be performed at first quite slowly in order to ensure precision of movement; and afterwards the speed must be increased, and the circle repeated continuously ten or twelve times.

PLATE VIII.

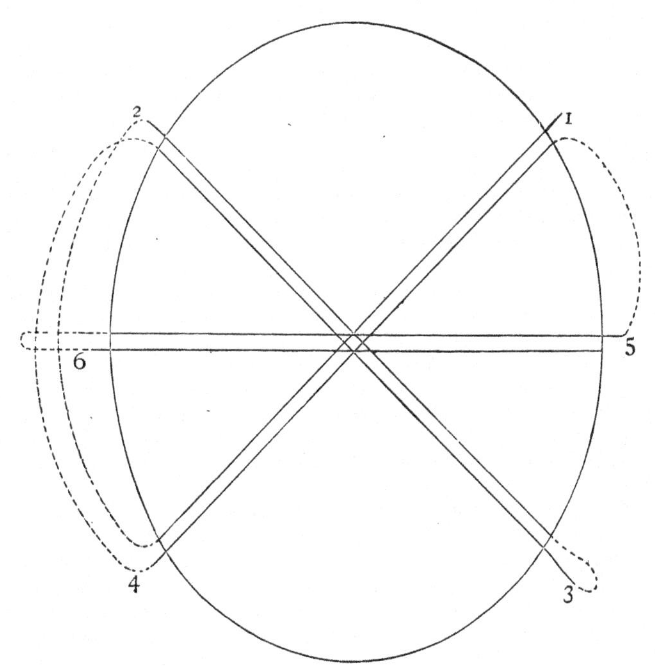

THE TARGET—AFTER ROWORTH, 1798.

Moulinet 2.

Motion 1.—Extend the sword arm, the hand to be in tierce, with the edge directed obliquely downwards from left to right.

Motion 2.—Drop the point diagonally down from left to right, and after the sword has passed its line on the target, allow the wrist to revolve until its inside is uppermost and the point of the sword to the right rear; complete the circle, and thus bring the sword again to No. 1.

Moulinet 3.

Motion 1.—Extend the sword arm, the hilt being as before about the height of the chin, the blade to assume the position of septime, the point being depressed about ten inches, and the edge to be directed obliquely upwards from right to left.

Motion 2.—Carry the edge diagonally upward from right to left, until it has passed the line on the target, then turn the back of the hand up, and complete the circle by dropping the point to the right rear, and bring the sword again to No. 1.

Moulinet 4.

Motion 1.—Extend the arm, the hilt being again about the height of the chin, the blade assuming the position of high seconde, the point being depressed about ten inches, and the edge directed obliquely upwards from left to right.

Motion 2.—Carry the blade obliquely upwards from left to right until it has traversed the line on the target, then allow the hand to revolve until the nails are uppermost, and thus continue the circle until the sword is again in the position of No. 1.

Moulinet 5.

Motion 1.—Extend the arm, the point of the sword to be directed about ten inches to the right, the edge towards the left.

Motion 2.—Carry the blade horizontally along the line on the target from right to left, and when it has passed the target turn the back of the hand up and complete the circle by passing the point of the sword over the head, in a position as nearly horizontal as possible, and thus come again to No. 1.

Moulinet 6.

Motion 1.—Extend the arm, the back of the hand up, edge to the right, and the point about ten inches to the left.

Motion 2.—Carry the edge horizontally from left to right, and when it has passed the target turn the nails up and complete the circle above the head, and return to the position of No. 1.

These moulinets must be performed with the wrist only and not with the elbow or shoulder, and will, if they are correctly practised, materially increase the strength and agility of the wrist, and they will moreover afford facility in leading the edge.

When this end has been reached, it will be advisable to combine the first four, i. e. the diagonal cuts in one continuous movement, which is sometimes called the "figure of eight": it may be found useful for defence at night, when, owing to the darkness, the movements of the enemy's sword cannot be distinctly seen.

The Cuts.

In this lesson, and those following it, it will be well for reasons of economy to substitute the single-stick for the sabre. The cuts should be performed not at the target, which should be only used for the "moulinets," but in a personal lesson with the master, and they might be further practised at a dummy or post.

Each cut is to be delivered on the full lunge, and whether the cut succeeds, or whether it is parried, the swordsman must for his own safety's sake recover instantly to his guard.

To attempt two cuts on the same lunge is bad swordsmanship, because it is dangerous, on account of the "riposte," or return hit, which a good swordsman is sure to reply with after parrying the first cut.

Cuts may be given with both the true edge and the false, or, as Lonnergan calls it, "the other edge;" but the latter I shall reserve for a special series of lessons for attacks on the sword-arm, in which it finds its chief use.

There are six principal cuts, which are based on the six moulinets, and they are directed at specified parts of the body, as follows :—

Engage in the *Medium* Guard.

Cut 1.—Deliver cut 1 of the moulinet diagonally downwards at the left side of the opponent's head, or his cheek.

On Guard.

Cut 2.—Deliver cut 2 diagonally downwards at the right side of the head, or his cheek.

On Guard.

Cut 3.—Deliver cut 3 diagonally upwards at the inside of the right knee.

On Guard.

Cut 4.—Deliver cut 4 diagonally upwards at the outside of the right knee.

On Guard.

Cut 5.—Deliver cut 5 horizontally at the left side or belly.

On Guard.

Cut 6.—Deliver cut 6 horizontally at the right side just below the ribs.

On Guard.

There are two other cuts which are not so generally useful as the above, viz. :—

Cut 7.—Deliver a vertical downward cut at the centre of the head.

On Guard.

Cut 8.—Deliver a vertical upward cut, with nails uppermost, at the fork. This is an Italian cut, which is used as a sort of substitute for the attack at the leg. It is a cruel blow, and should never be used in school play.

N.B.—Under certain circumstances, these cuts may be directed at parts other than those here mentioned: cuts 1 and 2 may be given at the leg, and when opposed to the high seconde guard, cut 3 may be given at the left cheek either above or below the sword, its direction in either case being parallel with the opponent's blade.

Opposition

Is the act of covering yourself with the shell in making an attack, especially on the upper lines, in such a manner as to protect yourself from a counter hit of the enemy.

The Point.

If the point be given *within* the sword the hand should assume the position of quarte, as the shell will afford protection against a time cut or a counter on the arm.

Similarly, if the point be given *without*, the hand must be in tierce.

The Pummel.

The pummel undoubtedly was used as a means of offence by the swordsmen of past generations. Lonnergan, who must be quoted as the representative master of the age of the English gladiators, plainly recommends it in the following words: "If the case requires the speedy chastisement of an insolent adversary, dart the pummel of your weapon in his face and trip his heels."

This is not an elegant movement, and should not be resorted to in schoolplay except under very exceptional conditions; but it might be useful to a soldier on service, when not much regard is likely to be paid to Fencing-room etiquette, and it should be executed as follows:

Should your enemy succeed in rushing in and closing with you, drop the point of your sword to the rear over your left shoulder, your sword hand being close to your cheek, and then force the pummel forward into his face.

THE DEFENCE.

THE "PARADE," OR PARRY.

HAVING described the attacks upon the various parts of the body we must now turn our attention to the means by which these attacks are to be met. These defences, or parries, are so very similar to the parries of the foil, that I shall adhere in my lessons to the names given to them in foil fencing.

Cut 1 at the left cheek may be parried in two ways, according to the position the sword hand may happen to assume: by *quarte* or by a *high prime.*

Cut 2 at the right cheek is parried by *tierce* or *sixte*, in the latter case the blow is received on the back of the sword.

Cut 3 is parried by a *low prime* or by *septime.*

Cut 4 is parried by a *seconde*, or by *octave* with the back of the sword.

Cut 5 is parried by *low quarte* or *prime.*

Cut 6 is parried by *low tierce* or *seconde.*

The vertical cut 7, if given at the head, should be stopped by the Head parry, formerly known as the St. George, and if given at the right or left shoulder, it may be stopped in the Italian fashion by a high tierce or a high quarte.

The vertical upward cut must be parried either by a septime, similar to that used for the Cut 3 at the inside of the leg, or by the Italian *horizontal quarte.*

There is yet another parry which bears a great resemblance to the "sword-arm protect" of the Angelo-Rowlandson exercise. It is used by the Italians to stop a return given over the sword at the right cheek after having parried an attack on the inside by quarte; it is somewhat in the form of a *high octave,* and by that name I shall call it.

Against the point the most useful parries are quarte, tierce, seconde, septime, and prime.

The parries must be executed as follows:—

Engage in the *Medium* Guard.

To stop Cut 1.

Quarte. Turn the hand to quarte, carrying it a little to the left, raising the point slightly, and receive the cut on the forte as near to the shell as possible.

High Prime. Raise the hilt, turning the edge upwards, and bring it over to the left front, taking care not to draw it in towards the body, the point to be depressed about six or eight inches, and looking to the front over the right wrist.

To stop Cut 2.

Tierce. Turn the hand to tierce, raising the point slightly, and carry the hilt a little to the right, edge to the right front, and thus receive the cut on the forte.

Sixte. This parry is only useful when engaging the "high seconde" with either sixte or octave. Raise the point slightly, and receive the cut on the back of the sword.

High Octave. Raise the hilt to a level with the top of the head, and by relaxing the grip of the second, third, and fourth fingers, allow the blade to drop forward as nearly perpendicular as possible, with the edge to the right front, and receive the cut on the forte.

This is the only possible parry for the return over the sword at the right cheek, and it will also stop the return at the right side under the sword.

To stop Cut 3.

Prime (low). From the tierce guard, drop the point forward, the blade to be nearly perpendicular, carry the hand a little to the left, the edge to the left front, and receive the cut on the forte.

Septime. From the medium guard, turn the edge to the left, carrying the hand a little to that side, drop the point in the form of septime, and receive on the forte.

To stop Cut 4.

Seconde. Drop the point to the right front in the form of seconde, and receive cut 4 on the forte.

Octave. From the guard in sixte, drop the point in octave, and receive on the back of the sword.

To stop Cut 5.

Low Quarte. Drop the hand about as low as the thigh in the form of low quarte, and receive on the forte.

Prime. Raise the hilt to the left front about as high as the shoulder, drop the point perpendicularly in the form of prime, and receive on the forte. This parry was known to the backswordmen as "the inside half hanger."

To stop Cut 6.

Low Tierce. Turn the hand to tierce, dropping it to the level of the thigh, and receive on the forte.

High Seconde. Raise the hand as high as the shoulder, lower the point so that the blade is nearly perpendicular, edge to the right front, and receive on the forte. This is the old "outside half hanger."

To stop the Vertical Cut.

Head Guard, or St. George. Raise the hand to the front a little higher than the top of the head, the elbow to be well behind the hilt, the blade pointing to the left front, and the point a little depressed.

High Tierce. Turn the hand to tierce, raise it to about the height of the right ear, and receive the vertical cut at the right shoulder on the forte close to the shell.

High Quartè. Turn the hand to quarte, raise it about as high as the left ear, and receive on the forte, close to the shell.

PLATE IX.

PARRY OF QUARTE.

PLATE X.

PARRY OF HIGH PRIME.

PLATE XI.

PARRY OF TIERCE.

PLATE XII.

PARRY OF SIXTE.

PLATE XIII.

PARRY OF HIGH OCTAVE.

PLATE XIV.

PARRY OF LOW PRIME.

PLATE XV.

PARRY OF SEPTIME.

PLATE XVI.

PARRY OF SECONDE.

PLATE XVII.

PARRY OF OCTAVE.

PLATE XVIII.

PARRY OF LOW QUARTE.

PLATE XIX.

PARRY OF PRIME.

PLATE XX.

PARRY OF LOW TIERCE.

PLATE XXI.

PARRY OF HIGH SECONDE.

PLATE XXII.

ST. GEORGE'S PARRY.

PLATE XXIII.

PARRY OF HIGH TIERCE.

PLATE XXIV.

PARRY OF HIGH QUARTE.

PLATE XXV.

PARRY OF HORIZONTAL QUARTE.

To stop the cut at the Fork.

Horizontal Quarte. Drop the hilt in front of the right thigh, edge downwards, and the blade directed horizontally across the body, and receive on the forte. This is an Italian parry.

This vertical upward cut may also be stopped by septime.

THE RETURN.

THE return, or riposte, made immediately after having parried a cut or thrust, and without shifting the foot or body in any way, is the most brilliant stroke a swordsman can make, since in making it he demonstrates his command of nerve in awaiting and receiving the attack, however subtle or however furious, and his activity in giving the reply, as well as his judgment in placing his hit on his enemy's person in such a way as to terminate the encounter at once—this latter of course has special reference to a combat with sharps.

The return is best effected from the position of guard, that is without moving the right foot, before the opponent can recover from the momentum of his foiled onslaught. Should it, however, not be rapid enough to catch him on his extended position, it must be supported by the lunge, and effected during his attempt at recovery to guard.

ADVANCED LESSONS.

Simple Attacks and their Parries with one Riposte.

In this lesson, when the master makes the riposte, he must cause his pupil invariably to stop it with the proper parry—but when the riposte is to be made by the pupil the master should mostly allow it to take effect in order to ensure its being made with completeness and precision.

To avoid confusion I shall designate the pair opposed to each other M. or master, and P. or pupil. I shall cause the master to commence the attack in each lesson, which must be afterwards reversed, the pupil commencing.

Lesson 1st, on Cut 1 parried first by quarte and secondly by prime (high).

M.	*P.*
Cut 1 at left cheek.	Parry quarte, cut 4.
Parry seconde.	
Cut 1.	Parry quarte, cut 2 over the blade.
Parry high octave.	

M.	*P.*
Cut I.	Parry quarte, cut 6 under the blade.
Parry low tierce.	
Cut I.	Parry quarte, point in quarte.
Parry quarte.	

Reverse the lesson, P. will commence.

Cut I.	Parry high prime, cut 4.
Parry seconde.	
Cut I.	Parry high prime, cut 6.
Parry low tierce.	
Cut I.	Parry high prime, cut I.
Parry quarte.	
Cut I.	Parry high prime, cut 5.
Parry low quarte.	
Cut I.	Parry high prime, cut 3.
Parry septime.	

Reverse the lesson.

Lesson 2nd, on Cut 2 defended by tierce and sixte.

M.	*P.*
Cut 2.	Parry tierce, cut 1 over the blade.
Parry high prime.	
Cut 2.	Parry tierce, cut 4.
Parry seconde.	
Cut 2.	Parry tierce, cut 6.
Parry low tierce.	
Cut 2.	Parry tierce, cut 5 under the blade.
Parry low quarte.	
Cut 2.	Parry tierce, point in tierce.
Parry tierce.	

Reverse the lesson.

Cut 2.	Parry sixte, cut 5 under the blade.
Parry low quarte.	
Cut 2.	Parry sixte, cut 1 over the blade.
Parry high prime.	
Cut 2.	Parry sixte, cut 6.
Parry low tierce.	

M.	*P.*
Cut 2.	Parry sixte, cut 4.
Parry seconde.	

Reverse the lesson.

Lesson 3rd, on Cut 3 defended by low prime and by septime.

Cut 3.	Parry low prime, cut 4.
Parry seconde (by disengaging over the enemy's sword).	
Cut 3.	Parry low prime, cut 1.
Parry quarte.	
Cut 3.	Parry low prime, cut 5.
Parry low quarte.	
Cut 3.	Parry low prime, cut 3.
Parry septime.	
Cut 3.	Parry low prime, point in quarte.
Parry quarte.	

Reverse the lesson.

M.	*P.*
Cut 3.	Parry septime, turn the nails down and cut 4.
Parry 4 by disengaging over.	
Cut 3.	Party septime, cut 2.
Parry tierce.	
Cut 3.	Parry septime, point quarte.
Parry quarte.	

Reverse the lesson.

Lesson 4th, on Cut 4 defended by seconde and octave.

Cut 4.	Parry seconde, cut 2.
Parry tierce.	
Cut 4.	Parry seconde, cut 1.
Parry high prime.	
Cut 4.	Parry seconde, turn the nails up, and cut 3.
Parry septime, by disengaging over.	
Cut 4.	Parry seconde, point tierce, above the sword.
Parry tierce.	

Reverse the lesson.

M.	*P.*
Cut 4.	Parry octave, cut 3.
Parry septime, by disengaging over.	
Cut 4.	Parry octave, point quarte.
Parry tierce.	
Reverse the lesson.	

Lesson 5th, on Cut 5 defended by low quarte and prime.

M.	*P.*
Cut 5.	Parry low quarte, cut 2 over the blade.
Parry high octave.	
Cut 5.	Parry low quarte, cut 6 under the blade.
Parry low tierce.	
Cut 5.	Parry low quarte, cut 4.
Parry seconde, or octave.	
Cut 5.	Parry low quarte, point quarte.
Parry quarte.	
Reverse the lesson.	

M.	*P.*
Cut 5.	Parry prime, cut 6.
Parry low tierce.	

M.	*P.*
Cut 5.	Parry prime, cut 4.
Parry seconde.	
Cut 5.	Parry prime, cut 1.
Parry quarte.	
Cut 5.	Parry prime, cut 5.
Parry low quarte.	
Cut 5.	Parry prime, point in tierce.
Parry quarte.	

Reverse the lesson.

Lesson 6th, on Cut 6 defended by low tierce and high seconde.

Cut 6.	Parry low tierce, cut 1 over the sword.
Parry high prime.	
Cut 6.	Parry low tierce, cut 2.
Parry tierce.	
Cut 6.	Parry low tierce, cut 6.
Parry low tierce.	
Cut 6.	Parry low tierce, cut 4.
Parry seconde.	

M.	*P.*
Cut 6.	Parry low tierce, point in tierce.
Parry tierce.	

Reverse the lesson.

Cut 6.	Parry high seconde, reverse the hand and cut 5 under the sword.
Parry low quarte.	
Cut 6.	Parry high seconde, cut 2.
Parry tierce.	
Cut 6.	Parry high seconde, point tierce.
Parry tierce.	

Reverse the lesson.

The Point.

The position which the hand should assume, whether that of quarte, with the nails upwards, or that of tierce with the nails down, when delivering the point, must be determined according to the guard adopted by the opponent, care being taken to oppose the shell to any possible counter or time of the enemy.

1st. Against the medium guard, when the point is given at the inner lines, the nails should be upwards, and when delivered at the outer lines, the nails should be down.

2nd. Against the sixte guard—here the inside only is really assailable, therefore the point must be delivered in quarte.

3rd. Against the "high seconde," the point should be given under the sword in tierce.

4th. Against the guard in tierce—here the upper outside line is completely covered, those open being low outside, and all the inside; the point must be given in tierce at the low outside, and at the inside in quarte.

These remarks refer especially to the initial attack.

I shall base my lessons for the point on the medium guard.

M.	*P.*
Point (quarte) at the high inside line.	Parry quarte cut 2 over the blade.
Parry high octave.	
Point quarte.	Parry quarte, cut 6 under.
Parry low tierce.	
Point quarte.	Parry quarte, point quarte.
Parry quarte.	
Point quarte (low).	Parry septime, cut 4.
Parry seconde, by disengaging over.	

M.	*P.*
Point quarte (low).	Parry septime, point quarte.
Parry quarte.	
Point tierce.	Parry tierce or sixte, cut 1 over.
Parry high prime.	
Point tierce.	Parry tierce or sixte, cut 5 under.
Parry low quarte.	
Point tierce.	Parry tierce, cut 3.
Parry septime, by disengaging over.	
Point tierce.	Parry tierce, cut 4.
Parry seconde.	
Point tierce.	Parry tierce, point tierce.
Parry tierce.	
Point tierce (low).	Parry seconde, cut 3.
Parry septime, by disengaging over.	
Point tierce (low).	Parry seconde, cut 2.
Parry tierce.	

DISTANCE,

Or "measure," is the exact space, taken in a straight line between the combatants, which must be traversed by the lunge.

Perfect measure, is when on the lunge, and without having previously moved the left foot, you can strike some part of the opponent.

Out of measure, is when it is necessary to advance at least one step in order to be near enough to touch the adversary.

Within measure, is when you are so near that you can touch or be touched without lunging.

"*Corps à corps*," is when the combatants have come so close together that it is possible for them to grapple with each other.

TO ADVANCE

Is to gain ground when the opponent is at too great a distance for you to touch him by the simple lunge; it is effected by stepping forward with the right foot about six inches, and then bringing up the left the same distance, so as to resume the proper position of the feet on guard.

To gain Ground on the Lunge.

This movement is only admissible against an opponent who has the habit of either springing or shuffling back when attacked. When on the lunge, instead of recovering to guard in the usual way, bring up the left foot until the correct distance between the feet is attained; and by this means make yourself master of the ground he has lost by his precipitate retreat.

In both of these advances take great care to preserve the erect position of the head and body, and to cover the movement by a proper guard with the sword, as some of the more skilful swordsmen are fond of throwing in a time cut on their enemy's advance.

To Retire

Is to give ground apace in order to resume perfect measure should the opponent have come within distance, or to avoid inconvenient pressure from an adversary of superior strength or impetuous temperament. In this case the left foot moves first about six inches to the rear, and is then followed by the right foot.

The retirement is sometimes effected by springing back from both feet; this method is rapid and covers more ground, and is advantageous in a room where the floor is level, but might be attended with considerable risk in the open.

A great many players of the present day, some of them even teachers of our art, are addicted to the vicious habit of rushing or shuffling back some three or four paces, without any consideration of what obstacle may be in their rear; and this they often do when attacked with but a simple lunge unattended by any advance; by this means they place themselves so far from their adversary as to be not only out of harm's way, but also out of the way of doing any harm. One who commits this error must be pressed and followed up by gaining ground on the lunge in the manner already described.

When a pupil evinces a tendency to this vice of rushing back, it is well to place him with his left foot touching the wall, so that retreat is impossible, and he must stand his ground, and either parry the attack or take the consequences. In the regimental fencing-room of the K.D.G. I found this method of cure a very excellent one

THE TRAVERSE.

This movement also is highly advantageous against one given to rushing back; it is of more practical use in the open than in the confined space of a "salle d'armes" crowded with fencers. It consists of shifting ground to one or other flank, in order to force the opponent to change his place, and of driving him into a less favourable position, so that he may have the disadvantage of light in his eyes, or may be embarrassed by finding broken ground or some other obstacle in his rear.

Traversing to the left is effected by moving the left foot about six inches off the line to the left, and then bringing the right foot opposite to it in the new line.

In traversing to the right, the right foot moves first, followed by the left.

Care must be taken to adhere strictly to these instructions in order to avoid crossing the feet, which would be attended with much danger.

The Pass.

This movement was in vogue regularly among the swordsmen of the ancient schools, even down to the time of the first of the Angelos, but it has since fallen completely into disuse among the votaries of the sabre and the foil, in the practice of which it is highly dangerous; it was used mainly in what was termed "commanding" either the person or the weapon of the antagonist. It is admissible, however, and sometimes even necessary, in the use of the sabre against the bayonet, and also in the manipulation of the short sword-bayonet or dagger, to which I purpose devoting a few pages.

It consists of stepping forward with the rearward foot, and bringing it a full pace in front of the other.

Commanding.

Commanding, that is to say, seizing either the person or the weapon of the opponent is, like its accessory the pass, regarded as obsolete in the modern fencing room, though in old times it formed a regular part of the system of instruction; and it seems to have held its own, on account of its usefulness, so long as the small sword continued to be a necessary part of the costume of a gentleman, and recourse to it undoubtedly saved many a life in the "rencontres" and sudden quarrels which were then matters of every-day occurrence.

Although this movement would be regarded as utter horse-play in the salles d'armes of the present, there is yet one kind of occasion in which I think it allowable, and that is in the case of an opponent who rushes in so close as to be corps à corps with you, and attempts to scramble a hit in with his hand drawn back, either by stabbing, a most dangerous practice, or by slashing underneath at the legs; such rough behaviour, amounts in itself to something very like horse-play, and if persisted in calls for treatment of an exceptional character. Lonnergan, as I have before remarked, prescribes, as a remedy for a gentleman of this class, the darting of the pommel into his face; but I think his discomfiture may be attained in a more merciful manner by commanding at one and the same moment both his person and his sword in the manner recommended by de Liancour (1686), and thereby rendering him absolutely helpless.

It must be effected as follows: make a complete volte * or turn about on the toe of the right, bringing the left foot well behind it, and while so doing transfer your sword to your left hand, which must grip it by the blade, close to the hilt, then pass your right foot again behind the left, thus bringing yourself completely in line with him on his left side, and facing in the same direction in which he faces, at the same time place your right arm across his body, and seize either the shell of his sword or his right wrist, and with your left hand present your own point at his throat.

Timing

Is, as Roworth puts it, the exact and critical throwing in of a cut or thrust upon any opening that

* Instead of "Commanding," it is possible to effect from this "volte" a cut 1 across the face or neck, drawing the blade along so as to make the edge bite.

PLATE XXVI.

COMMANDING—AFTER DE LIANCOUR, 1686.

PLATE XXVII.

SLIPPING—AFTER ALFIERI, 1640.

The line A gives the alternative of a cut inside the face, and the line B that of a cut outside the arm.

may occur as your antagonist changes his position. For instance, if he changes from an inside to an outside guard, or from an outside to an inside, in a negligent manner, his wrist becomes exposed, and frequently his sword arm above the elbow; the same opportunity presents itself if in his feints he should suffer his sword to sway his arm, instead of making them lightly from his wrist.

A time hit must not be confounded with a counter, which consists in striking at the opponent at the time when he makes his attack, without making any effort to parry or slip.

Slipping.

This is a movement of very ancient date. I find it mentioned by Alfieri (1640), and its use is recommended by Godfrey, Lonnergan, Roworth, and Angelo.

As Roworth says, the slip consists of "withdrawing the part (arm or leg) at which the antagonist directs his cut, in order that his weapon, being deprived of the expected resistance, may sway his arm from the defensive posture, and thereby afford an opening for a cut."

M.	*P.*
Cut 4 at P.'s leg.	Springs up to 1st position, drawing his haunches well back, and delivering a time cut at the face or arm, or a thrust at the breast.

If the cut at the leg is delivered inside as 3, then the time cut must be also inside as cut 1.

Counter-time.

This is the action used to frustrate a time hit, by making a false attack with a half lunge in order to tempt the opponent to time, and then, after parrying his cut, continue the movement in the form of a riposte at the most convenient part, as follows :—

M.	*P.*
Make a half lunge, and feign cut 4.	Slip the leg, and cut 2 at the arm.
Parry tierce, cut 1 over.	

Disengaging.

This consists of quitting that side of your opponent's blade on which you are opposed by his guard, in order to effect an attack where an opportunity may present itself.

It is performed either by cutting over the point, or by dipping under the blade as in foil fencing.

It is advisable to disengage over for a cut, and under for a point.

Beating

Is a movement of force, effected by striking aside the opponent's blade, and thus acquiring an opening.

It is performed as follows :—

M. and P. are engaged in quarte, M. wishes to force an opening, so as to deliver cut 2 inside the sword, which is a very difficult cut to parry.

M. therefore turns his hand to tierce, strikes the foible of P.'s sword with the back of his own, forcing it off the line to his own left, and immediately delivers cut 2 at the right cheek.

P. to defend this must yield his point and parry the cut with high octave.

2nd. The pair are engaged in tierce, M. turns his hand to quarte, and with the back of his blade forces P.'s sword to his own right, and delivers cut 1 outside the sword.

P. must yield his point, and parry with high prime.

N.B.—These two Italian parries are the only protection against the above attacks.

Redoubling.

This is a renewed attack very quickly executed, when the opponent neglects to riposte after parrying; to effect it the foot must be withdrawn from the lunge a little, and a fresh attack made at a different part of the body, before the adversary has had time to collect himself and place himself on guard again.

The redouble must not be confounded with the "remise," which consists of two strokes given consecutively on the same lunge, and which is considered bad swordsmanship owing to the risk of receiving a riposte while the second hit is being delivered; which riposte would in a fencing match be considered effective.

The Stop-thrust.

(colpo di punta d'arresto).

This is useful against an impetuous rush on the part of the opponent—it is in fact a time thrust—and is performed by delivering the point at the opponent's breast or face, and at the same time sliding the left foot back until the position of the lunge is reached.

The Under Stop-thrust.

Another form of the time-thrust, under the name of "Passata sotto," finds great favour with the Italians; it is effected by sliding back the rearward foot, dropping the body as low as possible to the front and supporting it by placing the palm of the left hand on the ground, the sword hilt, in giving the thrust, being held high in order to afford cover.

PLATE XXVIII.

THE UNDER STOP-THRUST.

FEINTS.

A feint is a false attack directed against some part of the opponent's body with the purpose of drawing away his attention and his parry, while the real attack is made at some other part.

The feint should be made by a crisp quick motion of the wrist only, great care being taken that the arm should not be in any way swayed by the movement, as that would expose it to a time cut; and immediately the opponent answers the feint with his parry, the opening so gained must be attacked with precision and rapidity.

The swordsman, having selected the point at which to strike, must decide by what movement he can draw his opponent's blade into the most awkward position from which to recover in order to parry the real attack.

I now give what I think are the most effectual feints.

Feint			
Feint cut	1 at left cheek,	and cut	4 at leg.
,,	2 at right cheek,	,,	5 at left side.
,,	2 ,, ,,	,,	3 at leg.
,,	4 at leg,	,,	2 at right cheek.
,,	,, ,,	,,	1 at left cheek.
,,	5 at left side,	,,	2 at right cheek.
Feint point	quarte at face,	,,	6 at right side.
,,	,, ,,	,,	4 at leg.

It is a good plan to practise these at a dummy, say a post, or a sack filled with sawdust, and placed upright, taking care that the feint should be executed just before the foot rises from the second position (which would allow the time calculated for a real opponent to answer the feint), and the cut should be completed just as the foot touches the ground in the position of the lunge.

This is the only sure way in which the application of the feint can be accurately studied.

Lesson for the Receipt of a Feint.

The feint is a movement intended to deceive the eye and shake the nerve, and it is therefore necessary to train the pupil in such a manner that he may acquire the habit of not being attracted by it. The teacher should therefore place himself in just measure, and explain that he is about to attack a certain named part, using a feint (not named) in order to effect the opening, and this must be repeated until the hand ceases to be drawn towards the part menaced, and forms the parry for the real attack, after which the teacher should name and work upon some other part in like manner.

Double Feints.

These movements require more than ordinary agility, as the swordsman is a good deal exposed to a time hit while making them, but they have the advantage of, when well executed, causing much greater confusion to the enemy than the single feints.

Feint	1 and 2,	and cut	1 at face.
,,	2 and 1,	,,	2 ,,
,,	,, ,,	,,	6 at right side.
,,	2 and 4,	,,	2 at right cheek.
,,	4 and 2,	,,	4 at leg.
,,	1 and 2,	,,	5 at left side.

Lesson for Returns preceded by Feints.

M.	*P.*
1st. Cut 1.	Parry quarte, feint 4 and cut 2.
Parry tierce.	
2nd. Cut 2.	Parry tierce, feint 1 over, and cut 2.
Parry tierce.	
3rd. Cut 2.	Parry tierce, feint 1 over and cut 6 or 4.
Parry seconde.	

M.	*P.*
4th. Cut 2.	Parry tierce, feint 4 and cut 2.
Parry tierce.	
5th, Cut 3.	Parry septime, feint 1 and cut 3.
Parry septime.	
6th. Cut 4.	Parry seconde, feint 2, cut 4.
Parry seconde.	
7th. Cut 4.	Parry seconde, feint 2 and cut 1.
Parry quarte.	
8th. Cut 4.	Parry seconde, feint 2, cut 5 or 3.
Parry septime.	

The Sword-arm.

I think with the Italians that it is better to propound a special set of lessons for the attack and defence of the arm, that being the most prominent part, and therefore the most easily wounded.

The master should point out what parts of the arm are most exposed to attack in the various positions of guard.

Lessons for Attack on the Sword Arm.

	M.	*P.*
1st.	Disengage over, and cut vertically at the outside, striking the arm just above the gauntlet, raising the hand so that the arm and sword form an angle; by this means the point of the sword strikes free of the opponent's shell.	Parry tierce (strong).
2nd.	Disengage over and cut 6 at arm.	Parry low tierce.
3rd.	From tierce. Disengage over and cut vertically inside.	Parry quarte.
4th.	Disengage over and cut 5 at arm.	Parry low quarte.

With the false edge.

	M.	*P*
5th.	From quarte. Feint point at face, and cut under the wrist with the false edge.	Parry low quarte.
6th.	From tierce. Feint point at face, and cut under with false edge.	Parry low tierce.
7th.	Against high seconde ; keeping on the medium guard. Advance the point under the opponent's hand, and cut vertically upwards with the false.	Parry by sinking the hand and taking the cut on the shell—a kind of low tierce.

Time cut with false edge on attack at the advanced leg.

8th.	Cut 4.	Spring up to first position, bringing the hilt nearly to the posture of hanging guard, and drop the false edge outside the opponent's arm.

COMBINATIONS OF RIPOSTES.

These exercises are intended to lead the young swordsman on to the "assault" or loose play, and they consist of a series of groups of attacks, parries, and ripostes. They seem to owe their origin to Mr. John Taylor, the master of the end of the last century, of whom I have already made mention, and from whom Mr. Angelo confessedly borrowed his system of broadsword instruction, on which the Infantry sword exercise of 1842 was based.

"The ten lessons of Mr. John Taylor" appear not only in Angelo-Rowlandson, but also in the 1804 edition of Roworth's book 'The Art of Defence on Foot, with the Broadsword and Sabre.'

Each lesson of the series must be performed until the pupil makes the movements contained in it with sufficient rapidity and precision, the master commencing—it must then be reversed, and the pupil will lead off.

Series 1st, on Cut 1.

	M.	*P.*
1st.	Cut 1.	Parry quarte, cut 4.
	Parry seconde, cut 2.	Parry tierce, cut 1 over.
	Parry high prime.	

	M.	*P.*
2nd.	Cut 1.	Parry quarte, cut 4.
	Parry seconde, cut 2.	Parry tierce, cut 5 under.
	Parry low quarte.	
3rd.	Cut 1.	Parry high prime, cut 5.
	Parry low quarte, cut 2 over.	Parry high octave, cut 6.
	Parry low tierce.	
4th.	Cut 1.	Parry high prime, cut 5.
	Parry low quarte, cut 4.	Parry seconde, point over.
	Parry prime.	
5th.	Cut 1.	Parry quarte, point.
	Parry quarte, cut 6.	Parry seconde, point over.
	Parry prime.	

Series 2nd, on Cut 2.

1st.	Cut 2.	Parry tierce, cut 1 over.
	Parry high prime, cut 4.	Parry seconde, cut 2.
	Parry tierce.	
2nd.	Cut 2.	Parry tierce, cut 4.
	Parry seconde, point over.	Parry prime, cut 6.
	Parry low tierce.	
3rd.	Cut 2.	Parry tierce, cut 6.
	Parry low tierce, cut 1 over.	Parry high prime, cut 1 or 5.
	Parry quarte.	

	M.	*P.*
4th.	Cut 2.	Parry tierce, cut 5 under.
	Parry low quarte, point.	Parry quarte, cut 4.
	Parry seconde.	
5th.	Cut 2.	Parry tierce, cut 5 under.
	Parry low quarte, cut 2 over.	Parry high octave, cut 6.
	Parry low tierce.	
6th.	Cut 2.	Parry tierce, point under.
	Parry seconde, cut 2.	Parry tierce, cut 5 under.
	Parry low quarte.	

Series 3rd, on Cut 3.

1st.	Cut 3.	Parry low prime, cut 5.
	Parry prime, cut 4.	Parry seconde, point over.
	Parry tierce.	
2nd.	Cut 3.	Parry low prime, cut 5.
	Parry low quarte, cut 2 over.	Parry high octave, cut 6.
	Parry low tierce.	
3rd.	Cut 3.	Parry low prime, cut 4.
	Parry seconde, cut 2.	Parry tierce, point under.
	Parry seconde.	

	M.	*P.*
4th.	Cut 3.	Parry low prime, point.
	Parry prime, cut 4.	Parry seconde, cut 2.
	Parry tierce.	
5th.	Cut 3.	Parry septime, cut 4.
	Parry seconde, cut 2.	Parry tierce, cut 5 under.
	Parry low quarte.	
6th.	Cut 3.	Parry septime, point.
	Parry quarte, cut 2 over.	Parry high octave, cut 4.
	Parry seconde.	
7th.	Cut 3.	Parry septime, cut 2.
	Parry tierce, cut 4.	Parry seconde, cut 2.
	Parry tierce.	

Series 4th, on Cut 4.

1st.	Cut 4.	Parry seconde, cut 2.
	Parry tierce, cut 3.	Parry septime, point.
	Parry quarte.	
2nd.	Cut 4.	Parry seconde, cut 1.
	Parry high prime, cut 5.	Parry low quarte, cut over.
	Parry high octave.	

	M.	*P.*
3rd.	Cut 4.	Parry seconde, cut 3.
	Parry septime, point.	Parry quarte, cut 6 under.
	Parry low tierce.	
4th.	Cut 4.	Parry seconde, point over.
	Parry tierce, point under.	Parry seconde, cut 2.
	Parry tierce.	

Series 5th, on Cut 5.

1st.	Cut 5.	Parry low quarte, cut 4.
	Parry seconde, cut 2.	Parry tierce, point under.
	Parry seconde.	
2nd.	Cut 5.	Parry low quarte, cut 6 under.
	Parry low tierce, point over.	Parry tierce, cut 1 over.
	Parry high prime.	
3rd.	Cut 5.	Parry low quarte, point.
	Parry quarte, cut 2 over.	Parry high octave, cut 4.
	Parry seconde.	
4th.	Cut 5.	Parry prime, cut 1.
	Parry quarte, cut 4.	Parry seconde, cut 2.
	Parry tierce.	

Series 6th, on Cut 6.

	M.	*P.*
1st.	Cut 6.	Parry low tierce, point over.
	Parry tierce, cut 6.	Parry low tierce, cut 1 over.
	Parry high prime.	
2nd.	Cut 6.	Parry low tierce, point under.
	Parry seconde, cut 2.	Parry tierce, cut 5 under.
	Parry low quarte.	
3rd.	Cut 6.	Parry high seconde, cut 5.
	Parry prime, cut 1.	Parry quarte, cut 6.
	Parry low tierce.	
4th	Cut 6.	Parry high seconde, cut 2.
	Parry tierce, point under.	Parry seconde, cut 2.
	Parry tierce.	

Left-handed Swordsmen.

All the great authors, both ancient and modern, who touch on this subject, are agreed that the only real advantage which the left-handed man has lies in the fact that, owing to the very small number of left-handed people, the ordinary fencer has but few oppor tunities of crossing swords with one, while with the left-handed the case is exactly the reverse.

Should, however, two left-handed men be pitted together, they are certain to be puzzled to an extreme degree.

The most important writers advise that pupils should be taught to practise with either hand, after having of course learned the art with the right.

To further this object I shall now propound a few easy lessons for the exercise of left hand against right, and in order to avoid confusion I shall allude to the cuts by names instead of numbers.

In these lessons I shall make P. commence, using the left hand, M. using the right, and when the lesson is reversed, M. will lead off with the left, and P. will take the right.

P. (*left hand*).	*M.* (*right hand*).
1st. Cut at left cheek.	Parry quarte, cut over at right cheek.
Parry high prime.	
2nd. Cut at left cheek.	Parry quarte, cut under at right side.
Parry low quarte.	
3rd. Cut left cheek.	Parry quarte, cut outside leg.
Parry seconde.	
Reverse the lesson.	

P. (*left hand*).	M. (*right hand*).
4th. Cut at right cheek.	Parry tierce, cut over at left cheek.
Parry high octave.	
5th. Cut right cheek.	Parry tierce, cut under at left side.
Parry low tierce.	
6th. Cut right cheek.	Parry tierce, cut inside leg.
Parry septime.	
Reverse the lesson.	
7th. Cut inside leg.	Parry prime, cut inside leg.
Parry septime.	
8th. Cut inside leg.	Parry prime, cut left cheek.
Parry tierce.	
9th. Cut inside leg.	Parry septime, point under.
Parry seconde.	
Reverse the lesson.	
10th. Cut outside leg.	Parry seconde, cut right cheek.
Parry quarte.	
11th. Cut outside leg.	Parry seconde, cut under outside leg.
Parry seconde.	

P. (*left hand*).	M. (*right hand*).
12th. Cut outside leg.	Parry seconde, point.
Parry prime.	
Reverse the lesson.	
13th. Point outside high.	Parry tierce, cut over at left cheek.
Parry prime (high).	
14th. Point low.	Parry seconde, cut at right cheek.
Parry prime.	
Reverse the lesson.	

Feints for the Left-handed.

Feint at	Left cheek,	and cut at	Right cheek.
,,	Right cheek,	and cut at	Left cheek.
,,	,,	,,	Outside leg.
,,	Outside leg	,,	Right cheek.
,,	Left cheek	,,	Inside leg.
,,	Inside leg	,,	Left cheek.

Returns for Left Hand, combined with Feints.

M. (*right hand*).	P. (*left hand*).
1st. Cut left cheek.	Parry tierce, feint right cheek, cut left side.
,, ,,	Parry tierce, feint right cheek, cut inside leg.
,, ,,	Parry tierce, feint right cheek, cut outside leg.

	M. (*right hand*).	*P.* (*left hand*).
2nd.	Cut right cheek.	Parry quarte, feint inside leg, cut left cheek.
	,, ,,	Parry quarte, feint left cheek, cut right cheek.
	,, ,,	Parry quarte, feint left cheek, cut outside leg.
3rd.	Cut inside leg.	Parry prime, feint outside leg, cut right cheek.
	,, ,,	Parry prime, feint right cheek, cut outside leg.
4th.	Cut outside leg.	Parry seconde, feint left cheek, cut outside leg.
	,, ,,	Parry seconde, feint left cheek, cut inside leg.

Combinations for Left Hand against Right Hand.

Left hand commencing.

	P. (*left hana*).	*M.* (*right hand*).
1st.	Cut right cheek.	Parry tierce, cut inside leg.
	Parry septime, cut right cheek.	Parry tierce, cut left side.
	Parry tierce.	

	P.	*M.*
2nd.	Cut left cheek.	Parry quarte, cut right side.
	Parry low quarte, cut over at left cheek.	Parry high prime, cut inside leg.
	Parry septime.	
3rd.	Cut inside leg.	Parry prime, cut left cheek.
	Parry tierce, cut outside leg.	Parry seconde, cut right cheek.
	Parry quarte.	
4th.	Cut outside leg.	Parry seconde, cut right cheek.
	Parry quarte, cut left cheek.	Parry quarte, cut right side.
	Parry prime.	

Right hand commencing.

	M. (*right hand*).	*P.* (*left hand*).
5th.	Cut left cheek.	Parry tierce, cut under at right side.
	Parry low tierce, cut over at left cheek.	Parry high octave, cut inside leg.
	Parry septime.	
6th.	Cut right cheek.	Parry quarte, cut over at left cheek.
	Parry high prime, cut left side.	Parry low tierce, cut over at right cheek.
	Parry high octave.	

	M. (*right hand*).	*P.* (*left hand*).
7th.	Cut inside leg.	Parry prime, cut left cheek.
	Parry prime (high) cut left side.	Parry seconde, cut left side.
	Parry low quarte.	
8th.	Cut outside leg.	Parry seconde, cut left cheek.
	Parry quarte, cut under at right side.	Parry low quarte, cut over at left cheek.
	Parry high prime.	

The Salute.

In all cases of fencing before an audience it is customary to pay it, as well as the opponent, the courteous recognition of its presence by the movement called the salute.

Standing in the 1st position, bring the sword to the recover, and turn the body on the hips to the right, lower the sword point to the right front at the full extent of the arm, the blade to point diagonally towards the ground, the nails downwards.

Recover swords.

Salute to the left in a similar manner, but with the nails upwards.

Recover swords.

Salute to the front, i. e. to the opponent in like manner, with the nails upwards.

THE ASSAULT.

To Engage.

Having performed the salute, cross the blades, and tap them smartly together twice; then draw back the left foot so as to be out of distance, and come to guard.

To Acknowledge a Hit.

Fencers have various ways of doing this.

I think, however, the most effective, most complete, and most graceful method is that which was used in old times in the celebrated school of Angelo, as follows:—On receiving the hit, spring up to the 1st position, pass the sword into the left hand, holding the blade between the forefinger and thumb, about six inches from the shell, with the pummel to the front; at the same time extend the right arm, with the hand open and the palm uppermost.

The Assault.

The Assault, or Loose Play, is the exact imitation of a combat with sharp swords, in which the opponents bring into use all the manœuvres contained in the foregoing studies, each endeavouring to seize every advantage and opportunity to embarrass and deceive the other in such manner as to render his own movements effectual.

In making the assault with the sabre it is customary to avoid the use of the point, owing to the risk of inflicting serious injury with it.

In case of leg-pads not being used, the Continental practice of abstaining altogether from cutting at the legs must be adhered to. Similarly, when the single-stick is substituted for the sabre, and leg-pads are not worn, no cut must be made at the inside below the waist.

Avoid, if possible, making the first attack against any adversary, more especially a stranger, it being advantageous to act on the defensive, in order to judge of the enemy's reach, and to study his style and his temperament; and in such case to vary the parries as much as possible, and occasionally, as the opportunity presents itself, to make use of a time cut or stop thrust.

Should the opponent also be determined to remain passive, recourse must be had to making false attacks with a half lunge in order to cause him to defend, and thereby discover his favourite parries, and also whether he is addicted to retreating, timing, or countering.

After making an attack, whether successful or not, recover at once to the position of guard; and it is wise, during the passage of the foot from the lunge to the second position, to shelter yourself under the "Hanging Guard," this will secure you to a great extent from being touched by an honest riposte when your attack has been parried, and also from a foul blow given after you have succeeded in planting your hit, which latter is a matter of constant habit with some men who would fancy themselves highly insulted if their swordsmanship were in any way called into question. Others there are who make a practice of rushing forward within measure, and when they find themselves close to their opponent they draw back their hand and either stab him in the body, or slash underneath at the unprotected leg; and this they do without the slightest concern as to whether they injure their opponent for life or not, their object being either to score a hit anyhow, by fair means or foul, or even it may be, in the case of a match, to so disable the man that their victory over him is an easy one.

These uncouth people almost always expect to be treated leniently by their adversary, and seem to think that a mere "Beg your pardon," after each of a whole series of foul blows, is quite sufficient, but it is a poor consolation to a scrupulously fair fencer after he has been badly injured by them. They utterly ignore the rules and customs of gentlemanly fencing, and betake themselves to mere fighting of a nature scarcely creditable to a Whitechapel rough; and such being the case they deserve to be met, so far as decency permits, on their own ground; and the best medicine for them is either the pummel à la Lonnergan, or the seizure as shown by de Liancourt, which I have described before under the head of "Commanding."

Some fencers are addicted to making noises, by stamping with the foot, or even by shouting, in order, I suppose, to intimidate the enemy. This is a very foolish practice, since very few people are frightened by it; while, on the other hand, should the antagonist have allowed himself to become momentarily abstracted, such noise would recall him to his senses, while without it he might have been caught off his guard.

When it is possible, attack rapidly with simple cuts or thrusts instead of using a feint, as one movement is quicker than two. Besides, if you always attack with a feint your opponent will, if well trained, readily perceive that your first movement is a sham, and will most likely time you on it.

When the adversary attacks in a hasty, passionate manner, it is well to give ground to him a little, in order that his fury may expend itself; to trust much to the parry and quick riposte, and to favour him when opportunity permits with time cuts and thrusts of arrest.

If he is of a sluggish nature, a rapid direct attack will most likely succeed.

If he appears timorous, it is better to clear an opening by the use of a feint, as he may on your direct attack maim you by a counter hit caused simply by his nervous awkwardness.

Watch mainly the opponent's swordhand ; but it is well to observe also his face, the face being the index of the mind.

Equipment necessary for the Assault.

1. A stout leather jacket, with extra padding or layers of leather about the shoulders and elbows.

2. A helmet with the face wires sufficiently close together to prevent the penetration of the point of the sword.

3. A strong leg-pad, reaching well up the thigh.

4. A body-guard or apron of stout leather to protect the abdomen and thighs.

5. An arm-guard or detached gauntlet-top long enough to cover the elbow.

6. A pair of fencing-gauntlets to protect both hands.

7. I advise further a stout ring of indiarubber to be worn over the wrist of the fencing gauntlet.

THE GAME OF THE SWORD.

(LE JEU DE L'ÉPÉE.)

THE GAME OF THE SWORD.

(*Le jeu de l'épée.*)

THE fencing-sword bears the same relation to the foil that the sabre does to the single stick, being the exact reproduction in a harmless form of the fighting sword employed by the French in their affairs of honour; it has the same triangular and rather stiff blade, and the same broad, deep, bowl-shaped shell, which is so constructed in order to afford shelter to the hand and forearm.

In this volume my space is too limited to allow of an elaborate treatise on the weapon, and I must therefore content myself with drawing attention to the rules generally observed in this style of fencing, and with giving a few hints regarding its successful practice. Those who desire to study its details still further I should advise to procure 'LArt du Duel,' by M. Adolphe Tavernier, and especially 'Le jeu de l'Épée,' by M. Jules Jacob, which is the most clear, concise, and practical work I have yet met with.

I ought to add that I myself am indebted for what I know of the Fencing sword to three eminent masters, M. Thieriet, now of the Cercle d'Escrime in Brussels, and MM. Clouard and Vitale Le Bailly, our two professors at the London Fencing Club.

The fencing-sword in practice should be regarded always as if its point were sharp, and no movement should be risked which could not be attempted with a real sword.

In contradistinction to foil-fencing, in which hits are only said to count on a portion of the breast, every touch counts, which would, if the weapon were sharp, cause a punctured wound; and hits mutually given count to neither party, although one of them may have been delivered on the lunge, because both combatants are held to have been wounded.

I always regard sword-play as being a much fairer and more straightforward game than foil practice, having seen many foil-fencers indulge in somewhat unseemly tricks in order to escape being touched on the "place d'armes," such as twisting the body, or covering the breast with the bent arm; I have known, too, a man more than once deny a palpable hit in such an impudent fashion as to raise a laugh among the spectators; such devices in the case of a fight with sharps might well involve fatal consequences. In sword-fencing, the first object must be to avoid being touched at all, the second to give the opponent what would be a disabling, though not necessarily a fatal wound.

The Guard.

The combatants should come to guard, standing in the first position, with the sword-arm extended, the points of the swords only touching; the left arm may be raised as in foil fencing, or the hand may rest on the left hip as in sabre play. To assume the complete position of guard, the left foot should be retired so as to place each man entirely out of reach of the other. The body must be quite erect, any leaning forward of the head or trunk being highly dangerous.

The sword-arm now should be drawn back, the elbow being near the side, the forearm must be in line with the blade, and the blade should be held in a horizontal position, the hand and arm being immediately protected by the broad deep shell. It is better, I think, to avoid contact with the enemy's blade as much as possible.

The Attack.

I have sometimes heard would-be critics in England—who, be it remembered, are well aware that they are never likely to be in danger of meeting an opponent armed with anything more serious than the playthings of the fencing-room—ridicule our neighbours across the Channel for so often being satisfied by a mere prick in the hand or arm. They are wrong; for it is pretty well understood that those who cultivate the habit of attacking first the more advanced parts of the adversary are, as a rule, the most careful, cool, and highly skilled swordsmen; while, on the other hand, they, who attempt the dangerous practice of attacking the body direct, do so either from bad temper or from ignorance of the art. In a serious encounter it is not of necessity our wish to take our opponent's life, but first to secure our own safety, and then to terminate the combat in our own favour by disabling him, and I cannot imagine a more thoroughly disabling stroke than six inches of cold steel through the sword hand.

The attack should never be made on the full lunge, as with the foil, but with only half a lunge, and the thrust should be rapidly darted out, with a crisp stabbing movement, and the hand instantly brought back to guard.

It is wise then for the most part to direct the attack on the most prominent points: first, the hand and arm; second, the head, if the opponent stoops very much forward; and third, though very exceptionally, the leg or foot; but it must be remembered that in attacking these lower lines there is great risk of receiving a counter thrust in the face or breast.

When a thrust at the body is risked, which should only be done under peculiar circumstances, as, for instance, to take advantage of some palpable opening left by the adversary, or, after having cleared the way by means of a forcible attack on the blade; the recovery must be effected by springing back with both feet from the position of the lunge itself, with the point threatening the enemy. Jacob recommends the assiduous practice of this kind of recovery.

Parries.

I think the best parries are quarte and contre de quarte, sixte and contre de sixte, septime and its contre, and seconde or octave and their contres.

Avoid making more than one simple parry; if deceived, it should be supported by its contre, or by the corresponding parry in the high or low line, according to circumstances; for instance, we are engaged in sixte, I disengage, you parry quarte, I deceive it, you parry contre de quarte; again I disengage, you parry quarte, I deceive it, you stop my disengagement by dropping your point to septime.

The riposte may be given direct at the breast or face; the quarte parries command the largest target, both high and low, but some returns very difficult to parry may be given from sixte.

In the lower lines the parry of septime especially seems to me to disorganise the enemy's attack; on the outer line I prefer the octave, though I grant its comparative weakness, to the seconde, as in the seconde position the hand assumes a downward bias owing to the incomplete action of the biceps muscle in supporting the fore-arm, which renders it liable to be deceived and drawn down by a feint under the hand.

In receiving attacks on the advanced parts, a great deal may be done by shifting the part aimed at, as, for instance, the sword-hand; and this, I think, would be much facilitated by a little attention to the practice for the dagger or short sword-bayonet, which will be found later in this book. When hard pressed by a forward fencer, it is well not to make too many parries, for fear of becoming disorganised; it is better in such a case to interrupt the combat by springing back out of reach.

The stop thrust is useful against an enemy who rushes in; it should be given, according to Jacob, at the head only, and not lower, for fear of an exchanged hit, and, after making it, the swordsman should secure himself by jumping back.

SABRE AGAINST BAYONET.

SABRE AGAINST BAYONET.

HERE we have a contest between two very unequal weapons, which has been treated of by several authors, notably Girard, Roworth, Mathewson of Salford ('Fencing Familiarised,' 1805), and J. M. Waite, 1880; it is also mentioned by Angelo, in the 'Infantry Sword Exercise of 1842.' Of these the four former writers seem bent on demonstrating the superiority of the sword, whether broad or small; but I am of opinion that, given equal skill and muscular strength to both combatants, the bayonet as a weapon must have the advantage, owing to its superior reach and greater momentum. In earlier days the management of the bayonet was scarcely understood at all, if we are to judge by the remarks on the subject by the authors of the period, and by the few illustrations that are extant, and therefore it is not surprising that the sword, the art of using which was very highly cultivated, should have been considered the best weapon of the two. In these days, however, bayonet-fencing is, to a certain extent, practised, and simple as its rules are, it makes the bayoneteer who understands it a vastly different opponent to the man portrayed in Mathewson's plates.

As regards the swordsman, the best guard he can assume is the medium, as it is the central position for the defence of all four lines, the parries being tierce and seconde for the outer lines, and quarte and prime for the inner; the other parries are not of sufficient strength to be applicable in an encounter of this kind.

The bayoneteer is certain, if he understands his business, to keep his point to the front and either level or just a trifle below the horizontal line, and to attack with a time-thrust on every occasion that he sees the hand of the swordsman move from his guard. The momentum of his thrusts is such as to require a parry of great force, and this causes difficulty in delivering a rapid riposte with the sword; while, even when his thrust has been parried, the bayoneteer can recover control of his weapon instantly, and deliver a second thrust before the riposte can be made, except, of course, where he adopts the course of altogether quitting the hold of his rifle with his left hand in delivering his thrust — which some foolish persons recommend him to do.

The swordsman's best chance is, should his adversary raise his point a little, to command the bayonet with his sword in a high tierce position, thereby raising it still more, and thereon to spring forward passing the left foot to the front, and seizing the rifle with the left hand. Similarly, if the point of the bayonet be carried low and off the line to the swordsman's right, the weapon may be commanded in seconde, the pass forward made, and the sword used for cut or thrust; but it would be an awkward movement to bring the left hand across to seize the musket. If the bayonet's point be held high on the inner line, it may be commanded by quarte, and if wide of the low inner line by prime, in both of which cases the left hand must be brought into play, and the cut or thrust offered either on the pass or the lunge.

It must be remembered, however, that these ways of presenting the point are blunders which no skilled bayonet-fencer would be likely to commit except in a moment of abstraction, or when overcome by fatigue.

The bayoneteer, should he find his weapon commanded by the sword, and the swordsman advancing within his measure, will do well to pass rapidly forward with his right foot, and deliver a blow with the toe of the butt according to the system propounded in 'Bayonet-fencing and Sword-practice.'*

When the swordsman has succeeded in seizing the rifle he should only offer the cut or thrust, as it is a gross breach of good manners to strike a practically disarmed man, unless, of course, the bayoneteer attempts by struggling to regain control of his weapon.

* Published by Messrs. Clowes and Sons, Limited.

THE SABRE OPPOSED TO THE FRENCH SWORD.

THE SABRE OPPOSED TO THE FRENCH SWORD.

This exercise is largely discussed by Girard (1736), and is treated by Angelo (1763); Roworth (1798) also mentions it. These eminent authors evidently regard an encounter of this kind as what it no doubt would have been in their day, when the sword formed an integral part of a gentleman's dress, a "rencontre" or sudden quarrel between two hot spirits armed with dissimilar weapons. Such an encounter, though obsolete for all practical purposes, is nevertheless to be recommended as an agreeable diversion from the usual round of fencing-school work, and it is an admirable test of the skill, judgment and activity of the performers, being distinctly a game of the brains, instead of one of conventional rules.

The combatants must commence work out of measure, and attack the sword-arm and hand; and the small swordsman, being armed with the more fragile weapon of the two, must have frequent recourse to shifting and slipping, in order to save his sword from too frequent contact with heavy cuts from his opponent, although at times he will be obliged to parry with the strongest part of his forte in quarte, tierce, prime and seconde. The sword should be held level, with the hand and forearm well behind their shell, which will defend them from many a telling cut without their using the blade to parry with.

The sabre should be held on the medium guard, with the point nearly in line with the opponent's chin, and thus the "sabreur" will find that his hand and arm will be protected by the shell, while, if he becomes fatigued, he can easily drop his hand to the position of Resting Medium.

The "sabreur," if he intends making a vigorous attack, must advance under cover of the combined moulinet, or figure of eight (∞).

On this the small swordsman should give ground a little, threatening repeatedly with his point, and wait either until his enemy makes the real attack, or becomes fatigued with the violence of his movements, he should then deliver a rapid thrust or two at the sword-hand.

It is impossible to lay down absolute rules for an encounter between weapons so unlike, and anything further must be left to the swordsmanlike judgment of the men engaged.

THE GREAT STICK.

THE GREAT STICK.

I so name this two-handed weapon in order to distinguish it from the one-handed stick or "single-stick" in use in our fencing rooms, in which it is entirely unknown.

Its practice is employed in the Italian and French armies, partly to supple the men, for which purpose it is an admirable and highly interesting gymnastic exercise, and partly to lead to proficiency in wielding the musket and sword-bayonet.

The system of instruction in those countries is somewhat different; the Italian method bears a very close resemblance to the practice of the two-handed sword, as taught by Achille Marozzo in 1536, while the French grafts upon a portion of that ancient play certain movements analogous to those of old English quarter-staff. In my opinion the Italian is the preferable game, and I shall follow it in the main, introducing one or two auxiliary parries from the French.

The Stick.

The stick should be five feet in length, and made of stout rattan cane.

PRELIMINARY LESSONS.

First Position.

Or position of "attention." Face to the front, with the heels together, the left arm dropped easily at the side, and the right hand grasping the stick about eight inches from the butt or thickest end, the arm to be straight and advanced towards the right front, with the nails turned to the right, and the point of the stick resting on the ground close to the outside of the right foot.

Guard (in Three Motions).

Motion 1.—Raise the stick horizontally to the front, the arm quite straight, the hand as high as the shoulder, and the nails down; at the same time make a half turn to the left, the right toe pointing to the front and the left toe to the left.

Motion 2.—Lower the point, and by bending the right elbow describe a circle on the left of the body, and as close to it as possible, bringing the point again to the front with the nails up and the forearm close to the body; at the same time grasp the stick with the left hand immediately below the right, the point being about on a level with the eyes.

PLATE XXIX.

THE GREAT STICK—FIRST POSITION.

PLATE XXX.

THE GREAT STICK—GUARD (QUARTE).

Motion 3.—Bend the knees and bring the right foot forward to the position of guard in fencing.

When these three movements have been acquired correctly, the player must combine them, and come to guard direct from the first position.

This guard is in fact a *quarte*, as a parry made directly from it protects the inner line.

We now come to the change of position called by the Italians "Fals-guardia."

False-Guard.

On guard in *tierce*. From the guard in quarte, turn on the toes of the left foot, and retire the right foot about 18 inches behind the left, the left toe pointing to the front and the right toe to the right, at the same time pass the stick, without quitting the grasp with either hand, from the left side to the right, the left hand passing underneath the right fore-arm ; the point of the stick to be on a level with the eyes, the nails of the right hand to be down, and those of the left hand to be up.

Change from tierce to quarte, retiring.

Turn on the toes of the right foot, retiring the left about 18 inches behind the right, and come to guard in quarte.

Change to tierce, advancing.

Turn on the toes of the right foot, bringing the left foot forward and come to guard in tierce.

Change to quarte, advancing.

Turn on the toes of the left foot, bringing the right foot forward and come to guard in quarte.

The Moulinets.

As in the sabre practice, so here, the moulinet is the means whereby to obtain suppleness and agility as well as to acquire the method of directing the cuts.

The Italian school has a large number of these moulinets, of which I think only six are really necessary, namely, two diagonally downwards, two diagonally upwards, and two horizontal—from right to left, and from left to right.

The moulinets should be executed in the first position, that is, standing erect, with the legs straight and the heels together, facing to the front. They must be performed slowly at first until they have been correctly learned, when the pace must be increased, and the exercise continued eight or ten times.

PLATE XXXI.

THE GREAT STICK—FALSE GUARD (TIERCE).

PLATE XXXII.

THE GREAT STICK—PREPARE FOR MOULINET.

The rotatory movement of the stick is much assisted by a pulling motion of one hand, and a pushing motion of the other.

The moulinets are :

No. 1, diagonal down from right to left.
No. 2, diagonal down from left to right.
No. 3, diagonal up from right to left.
No. 4, diagonal up from left to right.
No. 5, horizontal from right to left.
No. 6, horizontal from left to right.

Moulinet 1.

Motion 1.—Extend the arms with the stick pointing to the front a little above the diagonal line on the target, grasping it with the hands touching each other, the left hand behind the right, and the nails downwards.

Motion 2.—Bring the stick down with a circular sweep from right to left along the line, causing it to pass close to the left side, and bring it again to the front. The grip of the hands should be relaxed as little as possible.

Moulinet 2.

Motion 1.—Extend the arms as before, the point of the stick being just above diagonal line 2.

Motion 2.—Describe a similar circle, the point traversing the diagonal line from left to right, and passing close to the right side.

Moulinet 3.

Motion 1.—Advance the arms and stick direct to the front, the shoulders, hands, and point to be in the same horizontal line.

Motion 2.—Raise the point, and by lowering it to the rear, describe a circle close to the right side, the stick traversing the diagonal line upwards from right to left, coming again to the position of the first motion.

Moulinet 4.

This must be performed as the last, only, that the stick describes the circle close to the left side, and passes diagonally up from left to right.

Moulinet 5.

Motion 1.—As before.

Motion 2.—Describe the circle horizontally, the stick traversing the line from right to left, and in the rearward half of the circle just clearing the top of the head.

Moulinet 6.

This must be executed as the last, only that the stick describes the circle from left to right.

The Attacks.

There are seven cuts, one point, and one thrust with the butt.

The cuts and the point may be made either on the lunge or on the pass.

The cuts are in the direction of the moulinets already described.

Cut 1 at left cheek or shoulder.

Cut 2 at right cheek or shoulder.

Cut 3 at left leg.

Cut 4 at right leg.

Cut 5 at left side.

Cut 6 at right side.

Cut 7 is a vertical downward cut at the head.

The point is given usually at the breast, the arms at their fullest stretch, without quitting the grip with either hand.

The thrust of the butt is given by throwing the point of the stick vertically backward, and delivering the butt full in the face. This is to be used, à la Lonnergan, on an opponent who rushes in too close.

The Parries.

Quarte. From the quarte guard, raise the stick with the point slightly elevated, the right hand being about the height of the left shoulder, and receive cut 1 at the left cheek.

Low Quarte. Drop the hands as low as the hip, raise the point a little, and receive cut 5.

H. H. (*high horizontal*) *Quarte.* Raise the hands a little higher than the head, and slightly to the front of it, carrying them as much to the left as the extension of the arms will permit, the stick being held horizontally over the head, pointing direct to the right, and receive the vertical cut at the left part of the head or shoulder.

Septime. Drop the point, and receive cut 3.

High Septime. Drop the point, raise the hands as high as the left shoulder, and receive cut 5.

High Prime.	Drop the point perpendicularly to the left front (the right wrist crossing over the left), a little higher than the head. This protects the whole of the left side.
Tierce.	From the tierce or false-guard, raise the stick with the point slightly elevated, the right hand being as high as the right shoulder, and receive cut 2.
Low Tierce.	Drop the hands as low as the hip, raise the point a little, and receive cut 6.
H. H. (*high horizontal*) *Tierce.*	Raise the hands a little higher than the head, carrying them as far to the right as the extension of the arms will permit, the stick to be held horizontally over the head and pointing direct to the left, and receive the vertical cut at the right side of the head or the shoulder.
Seconde.	Drop the point and receive cut 4.
High Seconde.	Drop the point, raise the hands as high as the shoulder, and receive cut 6.
High Octave.	Drop the point perpendicularly to the right front, the hands a little higher than the head. This protects the whole of the right side.

There are also three other parries which I have adapted from the French, which I shall designate, for the sake of convenience, the French left, French right, and French Head Parry, but they are in reality parries of the old English quarter-staff.

French Left. Hold the stick perpendicularly on the left front, drop the left hand as low as possible, slide the right hand about a yard up the stick and receive cut 5 or 3 between the hands.

French Right. Hold the stick perpendicularly on the right side, drop the left hand as far down as possible, slide the right hand about a yard up the stick, and receive cut 4 or 6 between the hands.

French Head Parry. Raise the stick horizontally a little higher than the head and well to the front of it, sliding the right hand up about a yard, and receive a vertical cut at the head.

These three parries should only be used on occasion when the incident of position renders the performance of the others difficult.

PLATE XXXIII.

THE GREAT STICK—PARRY OF H. H. QUARTE.

PLATE XXXIV.

THE GREAT STICK—PARRY OF SEPTIME.

PLATE XXXV.

THE GREAT STICK—PARRY OF HIGH PRIME.

PLATE XXXVI.

THE GREAT STICK—PARRY OF H. H. TIERCE.

PLATE XXXVII.

THE GREAT STICK—PARRY OF SECONDE.

PLATE XXXVIII.

THE GREAT STICK—PARRY OF HIGH OCTAVE.

PLATE XXXIX.

THE GREAT STICK—FRENCH RIGHT AND LEFT PARRY.

PLATE XL.

THE GREAT STICK—FRENCH HEAD PARRY.

LESSON WITH ONE RIPOSTE.

M.	*P.*
Cut 1.	Parry quarte, cut 2 over.
Parry high octave.	
Cut 1.	Parry quarte, cut 4.
Parry high octave.	
Reverse the lesson.	

M.	*P.*
Cut 2.	Parry tierce, cut 5 or 3.
Parry septime.	
Cut 2.	Parry tierce, cut 1 over.
High prime.	
Reverse the lesson.	

M.	*P.*
Cut 3.	Parry septime, cut 1.
Parry quarte.	
Cut 3.	Parry septime, cut 4 under.
Parry seconde (passing back).	
Reverse the lesson.	

M.	*P.*
Cut 4.	Parry seconde, cut 2.
Parry tierce.	
Cut 4.	Parry seconde, cut 3 under.
Parry septime (passing back).	
Reverse the lesson.	

M.	*P.*
Cut 5.	Parry low quarte, cut 2 over.
Parry high octave.	
Cut 5.	Parry low quarte, cut 4.
Parry French right.	

Cut 6.	Parry low tierce, cut 1.
High prime.	
Cut 6.	Low tierce, cut 3.
Parry French left.	

COMBINATIONS OF THREE RIPOSTES.

Cut 1.	Parry quarte, cut 2 over.
Parry high octave, cut 6.	Low tierce, cut 1 over.
Parry high prime.	
Cut 1.	Parry quarte, cut 4 under.
Parry high octave, cut 2.	Parry tierce, cut 5.
Parry low quarte.	

Cut 2.	Parry tierce, cut 5 or 3.
Parry septime cut vertical at head.	Parry H. H. quarte, cut 6.
Parry French right.	

M.	*P.*
Cut 2.	Parry tierce, cut 1 over.
Parry high prime, cut 5.	Parry low quarte, cut 2 over.
Parry high octave.	

M.	*P.*
Cut 3.	Parry septime, cut 1.
Parry quarte, cut 6.	Parry low tierce, cut 1 over.
Parry high prime.	

M.	*P.*
Cut 3.	Parry septime, cut 4 under.
Parry seconde, cut vertical head.	Parry H. H. Tierce, cut 5.
Parry low quarte.	

M.	*P.*
Cut 4.	Parry seconde, cut 2.
Parry tierce, cut 5 under.	Parry low quarte, point.
Parry quarte.	

M.	*P.*
Cut 4.	Parry seconde, cut 3 under.
Parry septime, point.	Parry quarte, cut 6 under.
Parry low tierce.	

M.	*P.*
Cut 5.	Parry low quarte, cut 4.
Parry French right, cut 2.	Parry tierce, cut 5.
Parry French left.	

M.	*P.*
Cut 5.	Parry low quarte, cut 2 over.
Parry high octave, cut 6.	Parry French right, cut 1 over.
Parry high prime.	

Cut 6.	Parry low tierce, cut 1 over.
Parry high prime, cut 5.	Parry French left, cut 2 over.
Parry high octave.	
Cut 6.	Parry low tierce, cut 3.
Parry French left, cut 2 over.	Parry high octave, cut vertical head.
French head parry.	

THE
CONSTABLE'S TRUNCHEON.

THE CONSTABLE'S TRUNCHEON.

[This Chapter is specially dedicated to my late Comrades the "Specials" in 1887.—THE AUTHOR.]

IT must be remembered that the movements of weapons such as this are very quick, owing to their lightness, and for this reason it is necessary to keep the eye constantly on the opponent's right hand; by reason also of their shortness, and the entire absence of any protection to the hand, it will be found nearly impossible to use them for the purpose of parrying a blow, and therefore recourse must be had to the left hand to seize his arm, or grip him in some other way.

In practising, when it is necessary to stop a stroke, a rule must be made to seize the *wrist* and not the weapon. The enemy, in real earnest, would be a rough, or some such low rascal, who might be armed with a knife, or other sharp instrument, to lay hold of which would be disastrous; and great care must be taken to avoid stopping any stroke with the left forearm, for unless it were protected by some kind of defensive armour, it would most assuredly be disabled.

It is essential to consider on what parts a blow may be most advantageously planted in order to terminate the fight at once. A blow on the side of the head with a stout truncheon would very likely prove fatal, and I should not advise its use except in case of very extreme necessity, and an upward cut at the point of the jaw would be nearly as conclusive.

The best points to strike at, are those where bone is prominent, such as the collar-bone, the point of the shoulder, the elbow and forearm, the right hand, and, which might perhaps be overlooked, the advanced knee either inside or outside—but should this be attempted, great care must be taken to avoid a counter on the head; a thrust at close quarters in the pit of the stomach would be effective, and the pummel might be applied on the head or face.

The left hand can of course be brought into play for offensive purposes as in boxing, but I should prefer to reserve it for defence.

The truncheon should be held with the arm drawn back, and the hand near the body, in order to keep it out of the way of a stroke from the enemy's weapon, and should such a blow be attempted, the hand must be slipped or shifted, and a return hit delivered immediately.

In like manner the left hand also should be held rather back, and kept in readiness to pounce on the adversary's wrist.

When a blow is given it should be delivered with a

forward, and not a downward movement, in order to avoid the risk of having the arm seized by the opponent; in many cases a sufficiently forcible stroke can be effected simply from the wrist.

To facilitate practice, I advise the use of a dummy truncheon, consisting of a leather bag the size and shape of the real one, with a piece of rattan in the centre, and filled in with curled hair not too tightly packed; a pair of these dummies has been tried at the London Fencing Club, and found to answer their purpose remarkably well.

THE
SHORT SWORD-BAYONET,
OR DAGGER.

THE SHORT SWORD-BAYONET, OR DAGGER.

THIS weapon is to all intents and purposes a dagger, and the dagger we used to deem an arm of the past, belonging to no later period than that of our Tudor Sovereigns; now, however, that it is the intention of our military authorities to arm the soldier with a weapon of this kind, it is well to consider how it may be handled, with or without the musket. In my former work, "Bayonet-fencing and Sword practice," I have already discussed this arm as attached to the rifle, and therefore shall not further allude to that phase of its treatment; what we now have to think of is the bayonet-dagger wielded as a weapon by itself. Among civilised nations the dagger is an arm so entirely out of use, that in order to ascertain something of its capabilities as regards attack and defence, we must go back to the days when it formed part of every private man's personal equipment.

In the time of the Tudors the sword was, as later, the distinct appurtenance of the nobility and gentry, while the knife, or dagger, was carried by all, both gentle and simple. There are but few of the early authors—and I allude to authors of all the then civilised countries in Europe—who treat of the dagger by itself, though nearly all the masters of the 16th and 17th centuries recognise and teach its use combined with that of the old long rapier, to which it was a very efficient companion; of these Achille Marozzo, whose work first appeared in 1536, gives the most lucid description of its practice, and on his lessons I base the following suggestions.

There are two ways in which the dagger may be held, either *overhand* just as a sword is held, or *underhand*, which is exactly the reverse, the pummel protruding from the space between the forefinger and thumb; but I prefer the former. The ancients were accustomed to pass the forefinger over the cross-guard in order to obtain a firmer grip.

Engage, therefore, holding the dagger overhand in the medium guard, with the right foot advanced; the left hand must be open, and must be held close to the left breast, so as to be ready to seize the enemy's wrist.

The eyes must be constantly fixed on his dagger-hand, which must never be lost sight of, as the weapon, being short and light, is a very dangerous one; so says old Marozzo.

PLATE XLI.

THE DAGGER—GUARD.

M.	*P.*
	1st Lesson.
Thrust at hand.	Raise the hand to avoid the thrust and cut 2 at face.
Parry tierce, pass forward, and seize the wrist outside, forcing the hand up.	Turn left about on the toe of the right foot passing the left foot back, with both shoulders to the enemy; this movement will twist the imprisoned wrist free, and any stab attempted by the enemy will prove futile. Retire four or five paces and come to guard.

This lesson shows the danger of forcing the wrist up when the arm is across the body.

2nd Lesson.

M.	*P.*
Thrust at hand.	Shift hand as before, and cut 2 at face.
Parry tierce, pass forward, seize wrist outside and force it *down*, giving point at breast or cut at face.	
Back to guard.	

M.	*P.*
	3rd Lesson.
Cut 1 at face.	Pass to left front, parry quarte, seize wrist *inside*, force it down and point at breast.
Back to guard.	
	4th Lesson.
Stab up at body from below.	Draw the right foot back a little, raise the hand slightly and time with cut 4 on the forearm.
Back to guard.	
	5th Lesson.
Thrust at breast.	Carries his hand low. Time cut under the wrist with false edge.
Back to guard.	
	6th Lesson.
Pass, seize wrist, keeping it down and give point.	Carries hand low.
Back to guard.	
	7th Lesson.
Cut either 3 or 4 at leg.	Shift leg, step forward again and cut 2 at face.

M.	*P.*
	8th Lesson.
Cut at leg.	Shift leg, and cut 3 or 4 at arm.
	9th Lesson.
Thrust tierce at inside of hand.	Shift hand, cut 4 at forearm.
Shift arm, cut 1 at face.	Parry quarte, pass, seize wrist inside, forcing the arm outwards, and deliver either point or cut.

Throwing the Dagger.

An attack may be made with the dagger as a surprise, during a combat, by throwing it at the enemy, to effect which it must be darted forward out of the hand, with all the force possible, from the position of guard; and on doing so it is advisable to take advantage of his disarrangement caused by your unexpected movement, by closing with him instantly and securing his dagger-hand, when the various operations of the seizure may be brought into play in the manner described in the following lessons.

There are other ways of throwing the dagger, but I do not think them applicable to the particular weapon now under discussion.

THE SEIZURE IN DAGGER PLAY,

or the Method for an Unarmed Man attacked by one armed with a Knife.

Marozzo again give the most copious instructions as to the mode of procedure in an encounter of such unequal sort; the matter is also touched upon by Salvator Fabris (1606), and by the anonymous author of the 'Art de la Lutte,' a Flemish work which appeared at the end of the 17th century, and is superbly illustrated by Romein de Hoogue.

I have selected a considerable number of Marozzo's examples, and think that a reproduction of his very graphic woodcuts will be both instructive and interesting.

Seizure 1.

The enemy attacks with his dagger overhand, attempting a high thrust; seize his wrist from the inside and force it back outwards and upwards, at the same time pass your right leg outside and behind his right leg, grasp the left of his collar with your right hand, and so throw him over to your own left.

Seizure 2.

The enemy attacks with the dagger overhand, stabbing upwards from below.

Seize his wrist from the inside, forcing it upwards

and outwards, pass your right leg behind his right leg; then grasp his leg inside with your right hand, and pass your head under his arm; you can then either break his arm, or toss him on to your shoulders and either throw him heavily or carry him away.

Seizure 3.

He attacks with his dagger underhand, attempting to stab downwards.

Seize his wrist from the inside, forcing it backwards and outwards, pass forward with your left foot, grasp his leg inside with your right hand, and so throw on his back.

Seizure 4.

He attacks with his dagger overhand, attempting either an upward thrust or the high cut 2 at your face.

Seize his wrist from the outside with your right hand, passing your left leg behind his right leg; at the same time place your left arm in front of his throat and throw him backwards to your own left.

Seizure 5.

He attacks with the dagger overhand, attempting either a high thrust or a cut 1 at the face.

Seize his wrist inside with your left hand forcing it

up, pass your right leg behind his right leg, pass your right arm under his right arm so as to encircle it within your own left hand, and so either break his arm or throw him.

Seizure 6.

He attacks with his dagger underhand, attempting a down stroke from above, to effect which he grasps your collar with his left hand.

Seize his left wrist with your left hand, pass your right leg outside his left leg, place your right arm across his throat, grasp him in front by his right shoulder or arm, so as to hinder the movement of his dagger hand, and so throw him over to your own right.

This seizure is of course the converse of No. 4.

Seizure 7.

In this example he is a little in advance of you, and attempts a backward stab with his dagger held underhand.

Pass your right foot forward, seize his wrist with your right hand, and his elbow with your left, forcing his elbow forward, and his wrist back.

Seizure 8.

This lesson is the converse of No. 7, as you seize his left arm instead of his right.

Seizure 9.

He attempts a downward thrust with the dagger held underhand.

Seize his wrist with your left, and also with your right hand, your hands being close together, draw his straightened arm over your left shoulder, and turn your shoulders to him ; you can then, if he does not let fall his dagger, break his arm.

This seizure is described and illustrated both by Marozzo, and by Romein de Hoogue.

Seizure 10.

He attacks with the dagger underhand, attempting a downward thrust, and in order to facilitate his action, grasps the centre of your collar with his left hand.

Clasp your hands together, raising them over your head, and bring the fleshy muscle of both hands down with all your force upon his arm ; this will at least disable his arm, and force him to quit his hold.

You can also free yourself by a blow of your fist outside his arm, to assist which you must grasp his wrist with your left hand.

Seizure 11.

He attempts a low thrust with the dagger held overhand.

Seize his wrist with your right hand, pass your left leg completely behind both his legs, and seize him from behind with your left hand by his beard, face, or hair, and so throw him to your own left.

Seizure 12.

He attacks low, with the dagger held overhand.

Seize both his wrists, drop backwards yourself on to the ground, draw his hands towards you, and by placing your feet against his body throw him behind you over your head.

Seizure 13.

This is the converse of No. 9.

You seize his left arm, that being the most convenient, drawing it over your right shoulder.

Seizure 14.

He attempts a downward thrust with the dagger held underhand.

Advance your left foot, seize his wrist from the inside with your left hand, and his elbow with your right, and force his hand back, and his elbow forward, and so disable his arm.

PLATE XLII.

SEIZURE I.—AFTER ACHILLE MAROZZO, 1536.

PLATE XLIII.

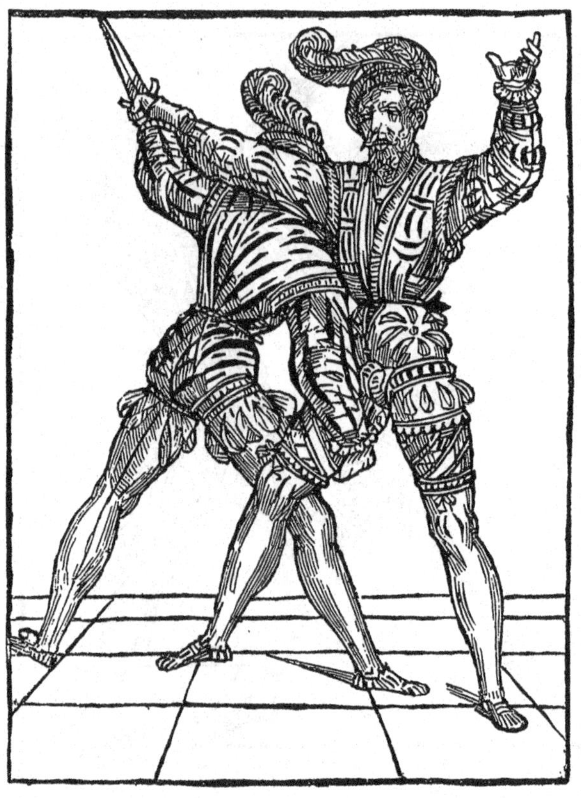

SEIZURE 2.—AFTER ACHILLE MAROZZO, 1536.

PLATE XLIV.

SEIZURE 3.—AFTER ACHILLE MAROZZO, 1536.

PLATE XLV.

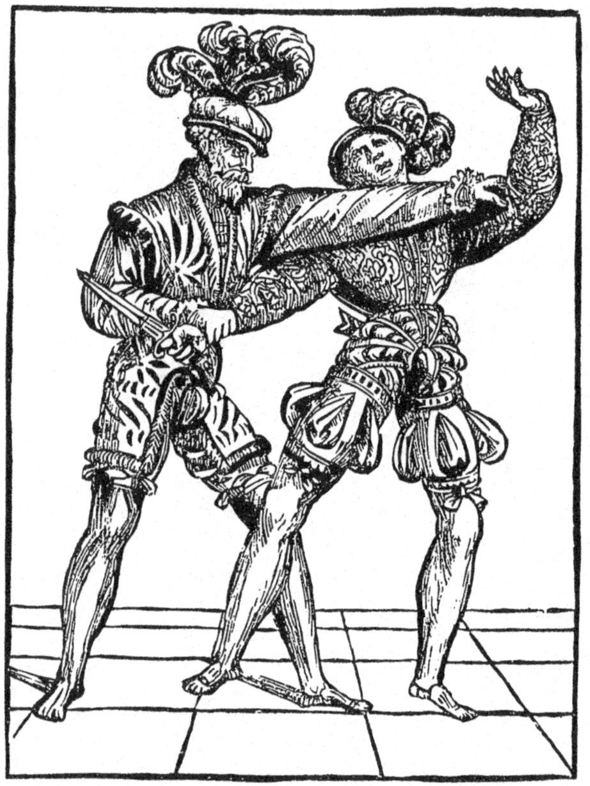

SEIZURE 4—AFTER ACHILLE MAROZZO, 1536.

PLATE XLVI.

SEIZURE 5—AFTER ACHILLE MAROZZO, 1536.

PLATE XLVII.

SEIZURE 6—AFTER ACHILLE MAROZZO, 1536.

PLATE XLVIII.

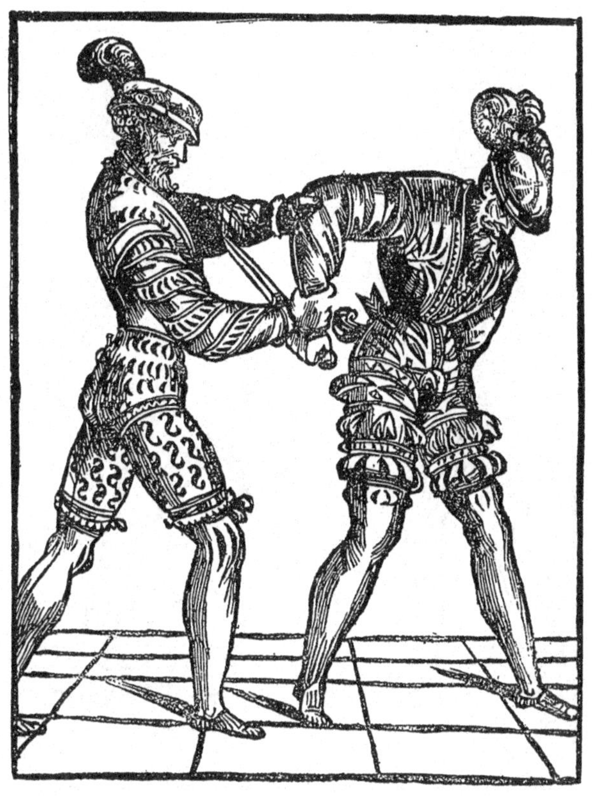

SEIZURE 7—AFTER ACHILLE MAROZZO, 1536.

PLATE XLIX.

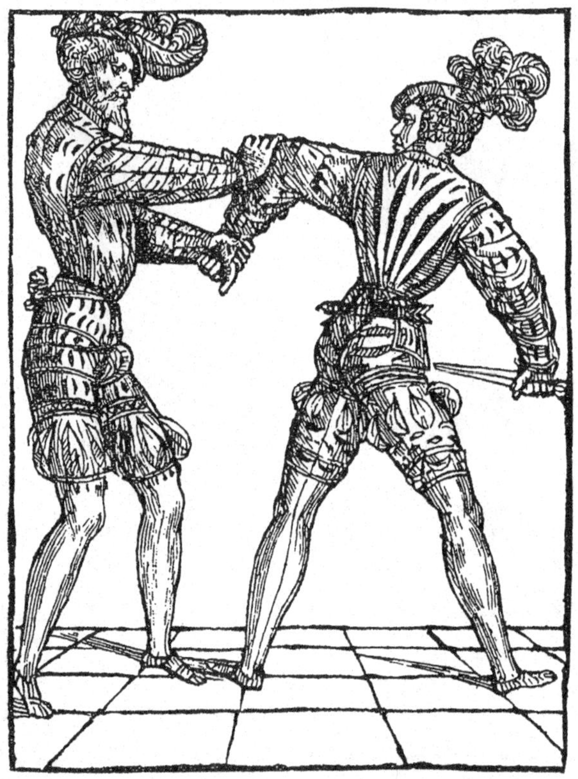

SEIZURE 8—AFTER ACHILLE MAROZZO, 1536.

PLATE L.

SEIZURE 9—AFTER ACHILLE MAROZZO, 1536.

PLATE LI.

SEIZURE 10—AFTER ACHILLE MAROZZO, 1536.

PLATE LII.

SEIZURE II—AFTER ACHILLE MAROZZO, 1536.

PLATE LIII.

SEIZURE 12—AFTER ACHILLE MAROZZO, 1536.

PLATE LIV.

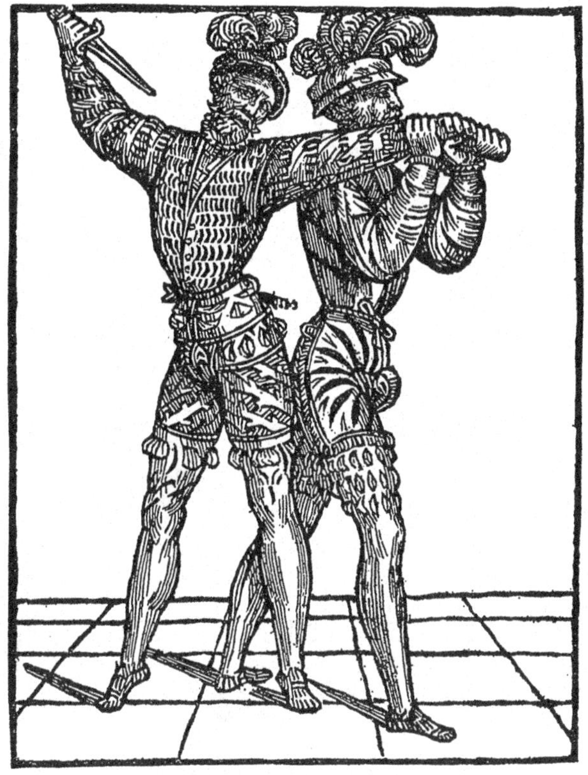

SEIZURE 13—AFTER ACHILLE MAROZZO, 1536.

PLATE LV.

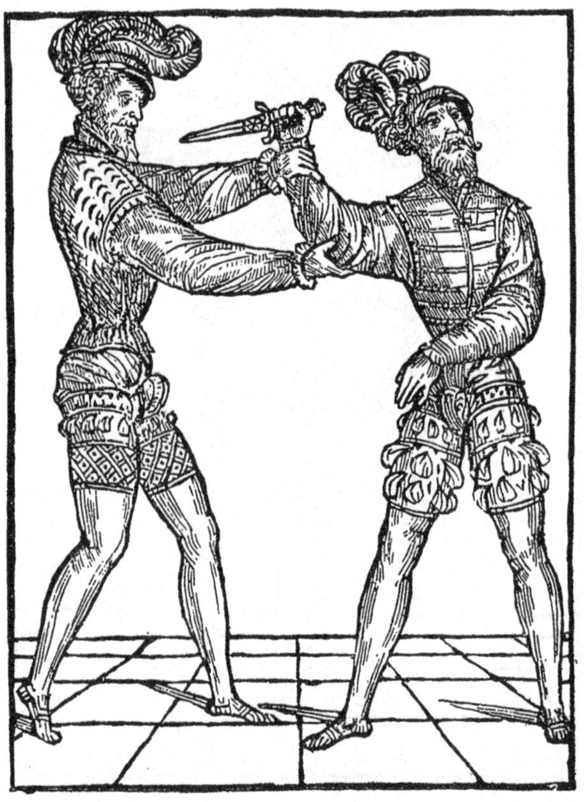

SEIZURE 14—AFTER ACHILLE MAROZZO, 1536.

RULES

TO BE OBSERVED IN THE ASSAULT,

OR

IN A MATCH OR CONTEST FOR PRIZES.

RULES

TO BE OBSERVED IN THE ASSAULT, OR IN A MATCH OR CONTEST FOR PRIZES.

1. The cuts and thrusts must not be given too heavily, hard hitting does not constitute good play.

2. With the *sabre*, *singlestick*, or *great-stick*, no cut is to be made inside, lower than the waist, unless suitable defensive armour is worn.

3. If both combatants lunge at the same time and both hit, the hit shall count to neither.

4. If both hit at the same time, only one being on the lunge, the hit must count to the one who lunges.

5. A pass in those exercises in which it is allowable is to be reckoned as a lunge.

6. With the *foil* the only hits which count are those which take effect on the "place d'armes," or that part of the breast on which it is agreed that they shall count.

7. *If, therefore, both lunge*, and both strike the "place d'armes," the hit counts to neither, but if one strikes it and the other touches some other part, the

hit must count to the one who has touched the "place d'armes."

8. If two hits are given together, the one being on the lunge (which is the fair direct attack) but not striking the "place d'armes," and the other striking the "place d'armes," but not being given on the lunge, the hit must count to neither.

9. If a combatant shifts his body, or shields himself with his arm or hand in such manner as to protect the "place d'armes" from being touched, and receives a hit on the part so presented, such hit is to be counted a good one.

10. Should a combatant touch by a *remise*, and at the same time be hit by the riposte of his opponent, the riposte is to count.

11. With the *fencing sword*, the play of which resembles an actual duel, all touches which would cause a punctured wound count as hits on whatever part of the person they may strike ; and if both combatants touch, whether on the lunge or not, the hit counts to neither, as in a fight with sharps both would be wounded.

12. When a hit is effected, the party receiving it must acknowledge in a suitable manner ; should he not acknowledge, but strike his opponent instead, the blow is a foul one.

13. After a hit is effected, both combatants must

retire to guard out of distance. Should either strike his opponent before coming to guard, such blow is a foul one.

14. A combatant giving a foul blow shall have one point for each such foul blow deducted from his score; and if the offence is committed more than twice, he must be disqualified from taking further part in the contest.

15. If a combatant is disabled, or his play in any way impeded by the injury caused by a foul blow, the party who has given it must be disqualified at once, as it is obviously wrong that he should be allowed to continue playing under an advantage caused by his own brutality.

16. If one should disarm his opponent, or if the opponent should lose his weapon *by accident*, it is considered courteous to pick it up and return it to him.

17. If a combatant lose his weapon during a rally or "phrase d'armes," and receive a hit without any pause or interval of time, such hit is a fair one; if, however, a pause should occur after the loss of the weapon, a hit then made is a foul one.

18. A combatant, dropping his weapon for the purpose of avoiding being hit, should have a point deducted from his score for each such action, and should this occur more than twice in the same contest, he should be disqualified for unfair play.

19. The left hand, and in the case of left-handed players the right hand, must not be used for parrying, opposing, or seizing the enemy's weapon.

20. A hit made with the sword held in both hands is not a good one.

Judges.

To decide the issue of a match there should be two judges and a referee, who must all be swordsmen of known competency; each judge should stand in such a position as to be able to watch one of the combatants, and as soon as that combatant receives a hit of any kind, he must stop the bout in order to decide its validity; and if there should be any difference of opinion regarding it, the decision of the referee must be final.

The presence of the judges does not absolve the combatants from honourably acknowledging a fair hit when it has taken effect.

In the case of a match or a contest for a prize, a copy of the rules should be supplied to each competitor as well as to the referee and the judges.

Copies of the rules should be hung up in conspicuous places in the "salle d'armes," as is the case in a billiard-room.

APPENDIX.

THE BLINDFOLD LESSONS ON DEFENCE WITH FOIL OR SWORD.

These lessons were imparted to me many years ago, when my Regiment was quartered at Aldershot, by a then eminent London Fencing master, who has since died, in order to further the instruction of my men in our regimental Fencing room, the superintendence of which our Commanding Officer, Colonel Pattle, had requested me to undertake. The master from whom I had them never published any work on the subject, although I often urged him to do so, and thus these lessons bade fair to become lost altogether; I found them however, of such superlative value in the training of the more intelligent of the young soldiers who came under my hands that I think they ought to be preserved for posterity.

The essence of these lessons is that the pupil is taugh, in making his parries to obey the sense of touch alone, for during the whole of them he has his eyes shut, the result of which is that the entire power of sensibility centres itself in the arm and hand, to such an extent that the nerves feel almost as if they were continued into the blade itself; the sensation of contact with the master's foil being as if a light magnet were being applied to one's own weapon; and therefore the moment this feeling of magnetism ceases, the pupil knows that it is time to form a parry, or series of parries, which have been previously explained to him.

As soon as his hand has become sufficiently dexterous in

thus forming the parries, he must be taught to dash out a riposte the instant he finds the opposing blade, with the extension of the arm only, that is to say, without lunging.

First Series.

On the simple parries of quarte and sixte.

The pupil when on guard in either of these lines must be made to cover that line completely; the master will then explain to him that on perceiving that the contact of the two blades has ceased, he must pass his hand to the parry on the opposite line and so find the weapon again, the master having disengaged.

When the blades are engaged, the pupil will close his eyes. The master will feel the pupil's blade strongly—not by pressure, but by moving his own foil up and down against the centre part of it, making the steel "bite," and this will cause that magnetic sensation which I have just alluded to; he will then direct.

On guard in quarte. Cover yourself. Shut your eyes.

On my disengagement, pass your hand to *sixte;* you have found me.

Cover yourself in sixte; I disengage, pass your hand to *quarte;* you have found me.

These simple movements must be continued until the pupil's hand passes readily from quarte to sixte, and from sixte to quarte, finding the blade each time.

SECOND SERIES.

Simple parries deceived, and the blade found again by a simple parry.

(A) On guard in quarte. Cover. Shut your eyes. I disengage; you parry *sixte.* I deceive you by disengaging again, drop your point to *octave;* you thus find me and arrest my second disengagement.

(B) On guard in quarte, &c.

I disengage. Try for me with *sixte,* I deceive you; try with *octave,* I deceive that also; bring your blade up again to *sixte,* and thus find me.

(A) On guard with sixte. Cover. Shut your eyes.

I disengage, you parry *quarte,* I deceive you; try for me with *septime,* where you find me.

(B) On guard in sixte, &c.

I disengage; you do not find me with *quarte,* try *septime.* I deceive it, and you will find me again with *quarte.*

THIRD SERIES.

Simple parries deceived, and the blade found again by their contres.

On guard in quarte. Cover. Shut your eyes.

I disengage; parry *sixte;* I disengage again, find me with *contre de sixte.*

We are now engaged in sixte. I disengage, parry *quarte;* I disengage again, parry *contre de quarte.*

FOURTH SERIES.

On the contres.

On guard in quarte, &c.

I disengage; you parry *contre de quarte.*

On guard in sixte, &c.

I disengage, you parry *contre de sixte.*

FIFTH SERIES.

Contres supported by simples and contres.

(A) On guard in quarte, &c.

I disengage, you parry *contre de quarte;* I disengage again, find me with *sixte.*

(B) On guard in quarte, &c.

I disengage, you parry *contre de quarte;* I deceive it, you parry *sixte,* and when I deceive that again, you find me with *contre de sixte.*

(C) On guard in quarte, &c.

I disengage, you parry *contre quarte;* I deceive it, you arrest my disengagement with *septime.*

(D) On guard in quarte, &c.

I disengage, you parry *contre de quarte;* I deceive it, you parry *septime*; I deceive that also, you raise your point again to *quarte,* and so find me.

(E) On guard in quarte, &c.

I disengage, you parry *contre de quarte*; I deceive it, you parry *septime;* I deceive that too, and you find me with *contre de septime.*

(A) On guard in sixte, &c.

I disengage, you parry *contre de sixte;* I deceive it, and you find me with *quarte.*

(B) On guard in sixte, &c.

I disengage, you parry *contre de sixte;* I deceive it, you parry *quarte;* I deceive that too, and you find me with *contre de quarte.*

(C) On guard in sixte, &c.

I disengage, you parry *contre de sixte;* I deceive it, you find me with *octave.*

(D) On guard with sixte, &c.

I disengage, you parry *contre de sixte;* I deceive it, you parry *octave;* I deceive that, and you find me with *sixte.*

(E) On guard in sixte, &c.

I disengage, you parry *contre sixte;* I deceive it, you parry *octave;* I deceive that, and you find me again with *contre d'octave.*

INDEX.